Inner Dynamics

Inner Dynamics

By

Sue Burnham

Here's Life Publishers

Published by
HERE'S LIFE PUBLISHERS, INC.
P.O. Box 1576
San Bernardino, CA 92402

HLP Product Number 951319
© 1986, Sue Burnham
All Rights Reserved.
Printed in the United States of America.

Library of Congress Cataloging-in-Publication Data
Burnham, Sue
  Inner dynamics

  1. Women — Religious life.   2. Women — Conduct
of life.   I. Title.
BV4527.B86   1986   248.8'43   86-9844
ISBN 0-89840-148-8 (pbk.)

Unless otherwise indicated, Scripture quotations are from the *New International Version* of The Holy Bible, © 1978 by New York International Bible Society. Used by permission. Other Scripture quotations are from The Living Bible (LB), and the King James Version (KJV).

FOR MORE INFORMATION, WRITE:

L.I.F.E. — P.O. Box A399, Sydney South 2000, Australia
Campus Crusade for Christ of Canada — Box 300, Vancouver, B.C. V6C 2X3, Canada
Campus Crusade for Christ — 103 Friar Street, Reading RG1 1EP, Berkshire, England
Lay Institute for Evangelism — P.O. Box 8786, Auckland 3, New Zealand
Great Commission Movement of Nigeria — P.O. Box 500, Jos, Plateau State Nigeria, West Africa
Campus Crusade for Christ International — Arrowhead Springs, San Bernardino, CA 92414, U.S.A.

To Mother,
the one who encouraged me to claim my
spiritual heritage.

Contents

FOREWORD

For me it has been exciting to see the ministry that the Lord has given Sue Burnham through her Bible study group ministry at Chapel on University Hill in Akron, Ohio, and as the wife of a truly outstanding pastor, Dave Burnham. She has touched the lives of literally thousands. As a qualified mental health professional, she has counseled many women who were at the extremity of their lives and who either were about to give up or had given up already. She knows what it is like to face low self-esteem with all its negative characteristics and to deal with its manifestations at the human level, but she also has seen what can happen when the Holy Spirit becomes the Inner Dynamic in the life of a woman. Sue herself is a living role model of what can happen when a person turns her life over completely to the great Enabler.

The material in this book already has impacted many lives through seminars and in audio tape form. I am delighted to see it now in printed form so that it can continue to minister not only to the felt needs but also to the real needs of struggling women. It will help women deal with those things most destructive to sound mental and spiritual health: low self-esteem, fear, anger, anxiety, bitterness, etc.

I commend this thoughtful and uplifting presentation of what it means to live with the Holy Spirit as the Inner Dynamic in your life.

Lawrence J. Crabb, Jr., Ph. D.

ACKNOWLEDGMENTS

I want to thank Les Stobbe for encouraging me to write *Inner Dynamics*.

My heart is grateful to Jean Bryant, Melinda Gipson and Bonnie Porter for their evaluation and editing of the material.

I wish to express my gratitude to Catherine Shipman for the countless hours she spent in the labor of typing the manuscript.

Each woman in my life has contributed to the contents of this book. I thank you all.

The names of most people have been changed to protect their privacy.

1
What's In Store For Women?

Claiming your spiritual heritage is the
dynamic for reaching your potential

It was one of my first Sundays in the church where my husband, Dave, began his ministry. I was twenty-one and a newlywed. My newly acquired titles — "Mrs. Burnham" and "pastor's wife" — indicated the changes going on in my life. Learning how to be a good wife was the enjoyable part of this new phase. The more difficult changes involved the other role.

I remember sitting in the oak pew that morning, still excited about the expectations of our new ministry.

Before the opening hymn, I felt a gentle tap on my shoulder. I turned, facing a middle-aged woman.

"Mrs. Burnham," she whispered, "I was wondering if I could talk to you after church. I'm fearful and having these crying spells at night. I need the help of a pastor's wife."

A pastor's wife at twenty-one. There I was, a scant two years beyond my teens, and I found myself faced with this dramatic adult situation. It was a year of transition for me. And it was abrupt. Anyone who has been married for more than a year remembers a few surprises after the honeymoon. That Sunday, I realized the role of pastor's wife wasn't what I expected.

Looking back, I see that I simply wasn't prepared for it, but this woman's problem compelled me to start searching. How could I help other women? The answer did not come overnight — nor in "ten easy lessons". But I did come to identify some vitalizing forces that transform women's lives. This discovery involved coming to terms with the past and future role of women.

A Lasting Impression

At twenty-one, all I knew about what makes women tick was what I learned from living with my female self, blended with what I had absorbed from my grandmas, aunts, sisters and, naturally, my mother.

I grew up with the security of a clearly defined woman's role, handed down by my mother's generation. That role had, in fact, served women well — perhaps since time began. It was simple. All a woman needed to do to be happy was to marry a loving man who provided for and protected his family. She, in turn, was expected to work hard to prove herself worthy of him.

I vividly remember my mother as a hard worker. I fondly recall the routines of her average work days. It was the mid-'40s, and as I look back, I see an attractive woman with a light wool jacket over her housedress. On this particular spring day she was taking advantage of the clear Midwestern weather, hanging clothes on the line outside. My sisters and I came home from school for lunch. Mother pinned up the last pillow case and followed us in through the side door.

Tantalizing kitchen aromas greeted us. Cooked ham and something sweet. Mother washed her hands, put on her apron, sliced banana over a cut-up orange, then sprinkled coconut over the top. Our ham sand-wiches, on two pieces of fresh white bread, were already prepared.

Earlier that day, after the breakfast dishes were done, Mother had walked the familiar two blocks to Sid's grocery store for the bread. Then she walked home to start the Monday morning wash. It was not simply a matter of pushing a few buttons. She tediously filled the washtub with water and shavings of bar soap, washed the clothes — white things first — rinsed them carefully, then pulled each piece through the wringer and hung them in the fresh spring air to dry.

In the midst of her washday, Mother found time to make a dessert. She had prepared baked custard, not from a pre-packaged mix, but from fresh eggs, milk and sugar. After we returned to school, she washed and dried the lunch dishes, scrubbing the crusted custard cups. Without television, there was no tempta-tion to put off folding the laundry in order to watch soap operas. The small radio in the kitchen was her only gateway to fantasy.

Life was the same for all the women in our neigh-borhood as it was for my mother. There was a certainty about their role — what they were responsible to do and on which days they were expected to do it. College degrees were as rare and unnecessary as fine jewelry. Instead of precious gems, these women valued their homes, families and morals. Their goal was to live an honorable life by being caretakers of these "valuables." Their reward was recognition and appreciation.

Ironically, most of my friends and I picked up the message from our parents that the added ingredient of a college degree would assure us even happier lives. So, we dutifully struggled for higher education and attained it. But, looking back, I believe most of us thought of our degrees as security — valuable in case of emergency. We simultaneously pursued our mothers' models of happiness. We relied on character qualities and lifestyle to prove ourselves worthy of a loving and responsible husband.

A Dramatic Change

Then along came the turbulent '60s. Within a decade the certainty of a woman's role began to fade. Dramatic changes took place. Students and young adults began to question traditions and values. Women spoke of freedom and personal fulfillment. Sparked by unrest over racial inequality, the media fueled a crusade for change.

A new frontier emerged. Women wanted to shake loose from their restrictions and push outward and upward from their "inferior" positions. They rebelled. In the '60s, many of their collegiate sons and daughters joined the revolution. Some rebelled silently, others openly. The 1964 Civil Rights Amendment crusade gave birth to feminism, legalization of abortion and the women's liberation movement. A new kind of freedom for us resulted, enabling women to choose alternative paths to happiness.

A New Breed

No longer was our only option the domestic life of scrubbing custard cups. The woman's role was irreversibly altered. Attitudes changed. Norms shifted. Popular culture increasingly came to equate domesticity with antiquity and servanthood. A new breed of woman emerged.

But with new freedoms came new problems.

James Dobson says:

> The traditional concept of femininity is being carefully and deliberately dismantled . . . . It appears that we have torn down the old value system before the new one was ready for occupancy,

> bringing widespread confusion and agitation. Thus, wives and mothers have found themselves wondering, "Who am I?" and then nervously ask, "Who should I be?"[1]

The clarity of a woman's role has shifted to a condition similar to an uncertain, overcast sky with a threat of rain. Self-doubt permeates the feelings of many a woman unprepared for a career outside her home. She judges herself, saying, "I'm out of step with contemporary women; how can I still find significance?"

Other women bemoan the fact that they must work outside the home for financial reasons. Society seems to insist on a standard of living that demands two incomes.

At the same time, the married career woman feels guilty for not spending time with her family. She may fear she's emasculating her husband. Then there is today's unmarried woman. She encounters difficulties with remnants of the past as she copes with chauvinistic attitudes in the marketplace. The unmarried, divorced or deserted woman with children often feels rejected. As one attractive thirty-nine-year-old divorcee expressed it, "No man would want me. I'm used, I've been married before, and I'm expensive because there's me and my children to support. Freedom? What's that? Unless a miracle happens, I'll always have to work."

A Current Dilemma

The stresses of contemporary women are real; our lives are complex and difficult. Is it any wonder so many fail to cope adequately?

The largest mental health survey ever taken in our nation provides disturbing evidence that these are indeed troubled times: " 'Nearly 20% of American adults,' a team of researchers from the National Institute of Mental Health reported . . . 'currently suffer psychiatric disorders.' "[2]

These results don't reveal what many feel in the pit of their stomachs but never confess to poll-takers. As a pastor's wife and a professional mental health counselor, I've learned that surveys reflect only symptoms of trouble — they're inadequate to define the depth of the feelings of women who are struggling merely to survive.

But the deep feelings eventually surface. When a woman feels unwanted or inadequate, she hurts herself. Like a sponge she absorbs others' comments and actions in a negative way. Then drop by drop, she squeezes the negative thinking out into her mind, focusing all her attention on it, and it reinforces her sense of a lack of worth and her inability to cope.

Today's woman feels inadequate to handle the demands and pressures of the new value system, and she finds herself powerless to meet the challenge.

In these changing times is there something that can help a woman pick up the pieces and put them all together? Are there inner strengths that make it possible for a woman to hum in good times and in bad times? Are there resources that engender positive feelings for a woman whether she works in a career or at home? These sometimes elusive elements — dynamics, I call them — are the vitalizing forces which bring about productivity and growth. They're the underlying morale factors which energize our lives. They're what get us out of bed in the morning and make us tick.

We yearn to become successful survivors — on the homefront and in the marketplace. However, a woman's life supports can be fickle, working sporadically and fizzling out or backfiring when the going gets rough. When this happens, she becomes anxious, depressed and angry. So she looks for a morale booster. A perfume ad promises: "Dare to discover your new image. Are you wildly exotic? Mysterious and alluring? Soft and romantic? Glamorous and dazzling?" It suggests that fragrances and cosmetics are the dynamics you need to make yourself desirable and attractive.

We buy and depend on these props to make us feel accepted, but we're misled. Such image accents fail to deliver. They do not hold a woman together during a personal crisis.

A New Direction

A crisis may creep quietly into your life, or it may come crashing down on you. Either way, you are driven to desperation. You feel helpless. Crisis is no respecter of persons.

Women from a variety of lifestyles have walked into my life. They have found open doors at our church, in our counseling office, and at our Bible studies. They have come searching for answers, needing help. And I have seen God do the impossible.

I've seen how a personal relationship with Christ can redirect and revitalize a woman's life. God gives strength in the midst of our weaknesses; He offers comfort in the midst of our sorrows. Whatever period of life a woman is in, she can be dealing with a crisis. Yet I've seen God change lives — often in the most unlikely cases.

There was Jamie. Tall. Slender. Jewish. With long, straight, dark hair. She was wearing an aqua blue wool dress. Unmarried. Early twenties, with a four-year-old son.

"I came to your church this morning not knowing a thing about it," she began, "to tell you about my unbelievable week and see if you can guide me as to what to do next."

She spoke rapidly. Brown eyes sparkling. Slender fingers brushing the air. "I've lived an evil, selfish life, pursuing my own happiness, but never attaining it. Instead I became more and more entangled with people and a way of life that disgusted me. Wednesday night for the first time I saw the ugly picture of myself and my unclean life. My half-drunk boyfriend lay on my bed, yelling obscenities and demanding sexual pleasures in the presence of my son. I was sober, fully aware of what was happening, and I surprisingly told him to get dressed and get out of my apartment. In an outrage he yelled and cursed me, but he left."

Her white face flushed with color. She sat back in her chair and took a deep breath. "It was so ugly to see how my boyfriend acted — horrible for my young son to witness that scene. And yet this is how I have lived since I was seventeen. Until Wednesday night, I never realized how corrupt I was. In desperation I got on my knees by my bed and cried out, 'Oh, God, if you are there, help me. I am so bad — I hate my life. Please forgive me. Show me another way.' "

She spoke with passion. She swallowed several times and smiled through her tears. "I slept so good Wednesday night," she whispered, and then continued, "On Thursday morning I awakened and felt clean. I knew I was a new person even though I didn't understand it. It was as miraculous as if my body were healed of leprosy.

"I searched my dresser drawer and found the Bible that a friend in high school had given me years ago. I read the book of John, all the way through. When I finished reading it, I was convinced Jesus Christ was the Messiah. Being a Jew, this was a dramatic moment. My heart pounded with excitement and I wanted to yell my discovery to the world. I picked up the telephone, called my mother, and said, 'Mother, I know you told me not to read the New Testament, and I never did until this morning. But Mother, believe me, you *must* read it. I *know* Jesus is the Messiah.'

"My mother replied, 'Who are you kidding, trying to tell me what to do — you with your messed up life?' And she hung up. I felt sorry for her, but the joy in my own heart was so exhilarating I knew nothing could destroy it.

"My boyfriend returned Friday night and I could hardly wait to tell him of my discovery and how we could experience a different kind of relationship. But he wasn't interested. He cursed me and walked out the door. Yet I still felt okay. I didn't feel desperate — like I *had* to have him. The joy remained.

"On Saturday I gathered all my clothes together and took them to my sister's house. I told her she could have them all in exchange for one dress. My clothes represented my former life. I wanted to put that life behind me and wear different clothes — to reflect the newness of my heart. She gave me this dress and I wore it to church.

"I found this church simply by looking in the Yellow Pages for a church in my neighborhood. I just wanted to tell you my news. I am a changed woman. I want to find out what God can do with my life and how I can teach my son how to live God's way. I hoped someone here would understand."

A Promising Potential

Jamie has a new dynamic inspiring her now. What are the pervasive dynamics of your life? Do you rely on your appearance or achievements or on another person to make you happy? Do you try to satisfy your needs by a combination of positive thinking and self-discipline?

A person's potential to accomplish something significant flows from God's Spirit within her.

This is a critical factor. The spiritual dimension is the vitalizing force behind a woman's approach to life; it's like the yeast in our bread, the battery in our children's toys, the energizing force in our everyday world that makes us hum. "This divine power has given us everything we need for life" (2 Peter 1:3). As a woman of God, you have a rich spiritual heritage.

My quest to uncover the secrets of dynamic living began when I was twenty-one. I've learned that there are distinct dynamics which vitalize a woman. These energizing forces enable her to experience her full worth and potential. No woman need be worrisome, depressed or resentful. Rather, by claiming her spiritual heritage, a Christian woman can be genuinely loving, filled with peace, joy and a sense of purpose. God offers you a deep transformation — deeper and more lasting than any magazine's makeover claims.

I don't promise that a dramatic cosmetic cure accompanies the practice of these principles, although your appearance will certainly be affected. Instead, I'll share some creative ideas for discovering the inner dynamics that release ongoing power, constantly available, whether you're scrubbing custard cups or practicing law. It's my earnest desire that you join me in this venture: discovering the true source of power for today's woman.

2
Who Am I Today?

*Establishing a relationship with Christ
is the dynamic for knowing who you are*

The fall air in Peking was crisp and refreshing, but I was suffocating. Everywhere I looked I saw masses of dark-haired Chinese people. They filled the streets and crowded the sidewalks — thousands of them, some on foot, others pedaling bicycles. Rising behind today's more modern sector, I could see the abandoned Forbidden City with its curving gold tile roofs and brightly colored buildings. In contrast to the vivid reds, blues and yellows of its past, the Chinese of the early eighties, post-revolutionary days were dressed in drab shirts and dark trousers. Their faces were somber. As I rambled alongside a never-ending river of grayish brown look-alikes, an ancient question stirred within me: *Who am I?* There I was. A lone American woman in western-style clothing adrift among the gray-garbed masses of the world's largest country. *Who am I*, I wondered, *in the monotonous life/death cycle of mankind?*

You may not identify with my intense feelings that moment in China, but as you flow with the routine of an ordinary day, do you ever question who you are? Maybe your career days are behind you, temporarily at least, and you're a full-time mother. As you bend over your baby to change a diaper or to tie your toddler's shoestring for the eleventh time, do you ever ask, Who am I?

This ageless question began to formulate in my mind years ago when I first started school.

My Name Is Important

My first-grade sister walked eight blocks with me to the large, ivy-covered, brick building where I was to register for kindergarten. I remember the excitement. But I also felt like a stranger when I entered the classroom. It was a stark contrast to the cozy, small Sunday school class where all the other five-year-olds were my friends. I worried, *Who am I among so many children?* I stood in a long line waiting to reach the teacher's desk. My turn finally came and I blurted out, "I am Sue Huffman. I live at 314 Altgeld Street." The teacher glanced up from the blue form, looked into my eyes and smiled. She calmly proceeded to fill in the blanks. My name had a magical effect — it identified me to the teacher. My name set me apart from every other child in the crowded room.

Years later, in China, my name identified me and set me apart. For what seemed like hours, I stood in line in the airport terminal waiting to reach the immigration officer's counter. He studied me, looked at the name on my passport, and then permitted me to enter his country. My name continues to be the constant distinguishing mark of who I am. It sets me apart from everybody else in the world.

Whether you like your name or not, your identity

is bound up in it. Your name spells out who you are — an individual, distinct from everyone else on this crowded planet.

What Do I Look Like?

What comes to mind when you hear your name?

When you hear, see or think about your name, a composite of various images enters your mind. Like a revolving kaleidoscope, these pictures of yourself move before your mind's eye, prompting various emotional responses. Everything you believe about yourself is reflected in this image. You probably visualize your appearance first. From seeing your own reflection countless times in the mirror you have formed a definite mental picture.

Do you see your artistic nose, your pointed chin or your chubby cheeks? I see my side profile first, then my dark hair and my freckles. What image do you see of your body? Too short, too tall, too fat? In our minds, we tend to magnify the imperfections of our body like we do our personality flaws. Our society emphasizes the desirability of a certain "look." Popular culture dictates that we're more than a skeleton covered by skin — the body size and shape is what matters. Advertisers promote the importance of a sexually attractive and physically healthy body. Physical perfection is the contemporary standard.

For some women, this popular ideal can develop into a driving force. Susan, a woman I occasionally play tennis with, plays several sets each morning five days a week, eats lunch, then spends the afternoon at the spa. Her life is energized exclusively by the dynamic of looking good and feeling fit. She permits nothing to intrude upon her vigorous schedule, certainly not a relaxing visit after lunch or a spontaneous shopping trip. As far as she is concerned, her value as a person *is* her body. The dominant picture of her fit form answers her Who am I?

You're so much more than a face in a mirror. Think again about your name and the multitude of images attached to it. The kaleidoscope shifts and family experiences and stories swirl together and add another dimension to the picture you have of yourself. Mental images of your father and mother flash across your mind. You can picture them saying and doing things in their peculiar style, using their pet expressions, or moving their hands a certain way.

Let an image of yourself come back into focus. You're talking in the same manner, repeating the same phrases or rolling pie dough with the same intensity your mother did. As I picture my mother's hands, I see her fluting the edges of the pie crust with exactness. Superimposed on that image, I can see my grandma's hands forming biscuits with the same precision. Then my hands come into view, with fingers and knuckles just like my mother's and grandma's hands, moving just like theirs.

I Feel Self-Worth When I Belong

As the kaleidoscope images of your mother and father blend into pictures of yourself, they stir mixed emotions. Self-esteem, or how you feel about yourself, is like the underside of a tapestry of your life. What do you feel as you visualize your mother and father? Do you have negative feelings toward family images? Or do they give you a warm sense of satisfaction? Much of the way you feel about yourself and your relationship with your mother and father is based on their acceptance of you.

How did your mother and father care for you? Are you aware that you were wanted? Hearing stories about your entry into the world and of your early childhood are one means of grasping your family's attitudes toward you. From words your mother penned in your baby book you learn about yourself and how other family members felt about you.

Stories like the one my mother repeatedly told me of an accident verified my value. I frequently asked her to tell it to me again. I've come to realize that it makes me feel truly special.

"You were a little girl, just twenty months old, and often played in the yard. The summer sun was very hot one day," she would say. "Your father decided to move his car under the shade tree. He did not know you were playing near the wheels. You fell into the path of the car when it moved forward and on impact your father thought he had hit a toy. Instead, he saw your limp, unconscious body. He picked you up, walked to the house, through the back door, down the stairs where I was canning cherries and handed you to me and exclaimed, 'I've run over our baby.' Frantically we rushed you to the hospital."

In minute detail she described each family member's concern as they cared for me during the critical days following. She always emphasized one point when she came to the part about my recovery. "God spared your life for a purpose," she said. I knew without a doubt that I was important to my family and I even felt a sense of purpose.

You may not have a personal story that draws you emotionally close to your family, but what about memories of special events that made you feel valuable? When your father, for example, asked just you to go with him on an errand, do you remember feeling special? I remember going with my father to the barber shop to get his hair trimmed and to the store to pick up supplies. Stopping once for a special hamburger treat at the coffee shop in our small town is still a vivid memory. It was my first hamburger and the best one I've ever eaten. I can still smell the pickles and feel the warm bun.

Do you have memories of snuggling up to your mother or father, perhaps as they read you a story or drove in the country on a summer's night? As you sat beside them, did you feel their warmth of love and feel a part of them?

If stories and memories are vague, how about the family photo album? It reflects your relationship with your family. Hopefully the album contains a photo of your mother, a look of concern on her face, holding you when you were a baby.

One of my favorite pictures in our family album is a hand-painted portrait of my older sister and me. Both of us are wearing organdy dresses with ruffles and matching hair ribbons. My sister's arm is draped over my shoulder in a loving, protective gesture. The picture depicts our mother's care for us and captures the message of being wanted and valued.

It also gives me a glimpse of my relationship with my sister, revealing that she cared for me. Knowing our mother and father and family members value us imparts to us a sense of personal worth. Their caring messages move into our minds and hearts and raise our self-esteem.

Maybe you didn't have a warm and supportive home environment such as I did. Maybe your parents didn't show affection or let you know they cared. A sense of worth then becomes even more important to you.

Peers Influenced My Self-Esteem

Throughout childhood the comments and actions of our peers contribute to our sense of being accepted. Negative comments, such as "You're fat," or, "You have ugly clothes," or actions that make you feel ignored and that belittle you, contribute to low self-esteem.

One woman confided to me the memory of her

embarrassment as an overweight twelve-year-old. She'd have given anything to evade Physical Education class. "I was especially awkward in the sixth grade," she said, "and my weight slowed me down even more. When the class ran relay races the girls moaned in disgust when I was on their team. But the teacher made it worse because she had stripped the shower of the privacy curtains. All the girls could see each other as they showered and the trim ones giggled and made comments about my fat body. I don't understand why girls are so cruel to each other. I can still feel the humiliation."

Teenagers' sense of being accepted by their peers, of belonging, affects their self-esteem.

Some teens will do almost anything to gain that sense of belonging, of being important to others. They may paint their hair blue, wear bizarre shirts, or put a padlock necklace on a chain and wear it around their necks. The more insecure a person is, the more reassurance he needs from others. A teenager's need to belong is so strong it can propel her to make decisions with long-range, damaging effects.

A beautiful seventeen-year-old girl sat in my office and confessed to surrendering her morals in order to be accepted. Linda sat on the edge of the sofa with her long legs crossed, nervously picking at her fingernails. She related her story of a downward spiral from insecurity to immorality to feelings of guilt. In a soft voice she explained, "My parents said they loved me, but it seemed they never had time for me. I felt rejected in school as a child and unable to identify with the group. When I was fourteen, I began using drugs like some girls were doing so I would be part of their group."

She stopped and reached in her purse for her hanky, then buried her face in her hands as she began crying. She continued her confession between sobs saying, "I am so ashamed. It's hard for me to say this." Finally she blurted out, "I accepted a living arrangement with an older man in exchange for a daily supply of drugs because I had no money to buy them." Linda paused and looked relieved.

Then she added, "I felt deceitful because I continued my appearances in church, and my parents never discovered my absences from home at night. I know what I did was wrong and I felt so guilty, but I wanted to be like the other girls so much, even when I hated the old man I slept with." She wiped her nose, cleared her throat and spoke calmly again. "I've met a wonderful young man who wants to marry me. I've broken off with the old man but I'm afraid of him." Tears flooded her eyes again when she said, "I've come to ask you, what should I tell the man who asked me to marry him? Should I tell him everything? Can I be forgiven?"

What an unhappy sacrifice! When you think back to your childhood and teen years, are you burdened with unhappy memories? Do you feel you've failed to find out who you are?

Contemporary music lyrics emphasize a lack of identity. Pink Floyd sings, "All in all, all we are is a brick in the wall." Then there are the lyrics by Prince: "Am I black or white? Am I straight or gay? Controversy!" Each of us needs assurance that we are more than just a brick. We have a basic need for personal worth; we need to know we have value as individuals.

What Blocks My Potential?

Establishing our personality by fulfilling our potential is also a basic need. Each of us desires a place of distinction in society — something that bears our own mark of individuality. We want others to know, *I was here.*

Remember the delight you felt when you learned to

skip, whistle or read? Developing these skills created confidence and enhanced your self- image. Each success was a springboard for testing more of your potential, continually bearing upon your self-esteem. You felt good about yourself whenever you learned, developed and finally discovered areas where you excelled.

Where is your potential? Is it in art, music, athletics, management, science? Fine-tuning a special ability creates confidence. Cultivating a talent in turn develops self-esteem.

Unfortunately, potential is thwarted by emotional blocks. Fear and conflict prevent a woman from developing her potential and learning new skills. If a woman is insecure she will fear others' comments and will dislike herself even more if she fails. So the potential lies dormant, untapped inside the one who is afraid to open the door which locks in the answer to who she is and locks out her feelings of worth.

Emily, a newlywed, struggled with several emotional blocks. She and her husband lived in a house trailer. She was relieved to move away from her family home, even though she now lived in a small space. All her life, her mother had targeted her as the scapegoat for her own frustrations. Now a timid-looking young woman with downcast eyes, she said, "My mother was either yelling at me, beating me or cursing me, telling me how bad I was or blaming me for causing turmoil. She demanded perfection and went into a rage if I didn't iron the collars of my father's shirts to her satisfaction. In my early teens I lied about my age and got a job at the supermarket after school just to avoid facing my mother and her abuse."

The emotional scars were deep; Emily had never released her feelings or negative experiences to anyone. After she married, her husband became disturbed by her nightly crying and insisted she seek help.

Domestic life was difficult for this small, brown-haired woman. She scrubbed her trailer each morning and again in the evening before her husband came home, making certain she did her job well. Her large blue eyes filled with tears and she tensed her mouth, trying not to cry, when she told me in a whisper, "I can't cook; there's just too much to learn about it, and I don't have anybody to teach me, and I'm afraid." She had just learned she was pregnant and said she was afraid to have the baby. Shaking her head, she said, "I don't know how to be a mother."

Feeling inadequate is as miserable as feeling that we don't belong; experiencing either creates insecurity. These unfulfilled needs often can be traced to childhood, but sometimes they appear in a more recent area of our development.

For many, the degree of respect or approval others give them determines the respect or approval they feel for themselves. As our physical body is reflected in a mirror, so we can look for our worth to be reflected in the eyes of others. In the quest for self-esteem and in an attempt to receive approval from others, we strive to measure up to society's ideal. Obsessively, we reach for the elusive essentials of self-esteem by struggling through self-improvement courses and searching self-help books.

When a woman doesn't measure up to Madison Avenue's definition of the ideal image, she might feel discredited. She might feel worthless even though she has average abilities or a normal family. This is tragic. If we continue to measure our self-esteem by society's ideal standards we will feel deficient in one area or another of our self-image.

This is a typical cycle. Women yearn to reach their potential — to become more beautiful, fit, intelligent. Yet in striving to reach an ideal, they are forced to deal with the reality of personal limitation. Each of us feels inferior in some aspect of our identity, our appearance, our family background or our abilities. This is normal.

Finding My Worth In Christ

Do you have good self-esteem? Is it because you're rated highly by society's standards, or have you found another way of establishing personal value? Let me share my personal discovery with you. Giving up and exchanging my pursuit of good feelings for a relationship with God is the dynamic — or vitalizing force — which transforms my self-image and how I feel about myself.

If I center my life on pleasing God, my self-esteem isn't determined by whether I'm average above average or below average. Rather, how I feel about myself is related to God's estimation of me.

Look at it this way. Shifting your focus from others to God can positively alter the way you see and feel about yourself. People tend to have variable opinions and fluctuating standards. When you trust the creator who designed you and make Him your reference point, you'll see yourself from His perspective.

A good place to start is Psalm 139. As we study His descriptions of us in the Bible, we find many expressions of acceptance and love. You can learn to rest in His acceptance instead of trying to gain the world's approval.

You are loved. Read Jeremiah 31:3: "I have loved you with an everlasting love; I have drawn you with loving kindness." God loves you so much that He sent Jesus Christ to free you from the bondage of sin, from slavery to others and their opinions.

Sin is defined as choosing to disobey God and go on in our own willful way. This results in separation from Him. For a full explanation of how you can respond to God's love and deal with your proneness to sin, see the appendix at the end of this book.

As I understand it, Jesus came to show us how to live. When you become a Christian, He makes it possible for you to align your values with what pleases God. When Christ died on the cross and rose from the grave, He paid the penalty for your sins. He died for you. 1 Peter 1:18,19 says: "For you know it was not with perishable things, such as silver and gold, that you were redeemed from the empty way of life handed down to you from your forefathers, but with the precious blood of Christ, a lamb without blemish or defect." This shows how precious you are to Him.

God Offers Me Security

Earlier, we reflected on our identity, examining the messages accumulated from our family photo albums — memories, stories and successes. But maybe you don't have any photo albums or family stories or personal successes. Maybe your memories stir up bad feelings of rejection by family or friends or both.

Or maybe your baby books are filled with reflections of acceptance, but you are hard pressed to recall any recent affirmations of belonging. When your family and friends aren't around, who tells you you're worth something?

Have you become a member of God's family? Does the prayer at the end of the Four Spiritual Laws express the desire of your heart? The gift of salvation is yours when you receive Christ. Right now you can turn from your sin and invite Christ to come into your heart and life, as He promised. God's Word says: "But as many as received Him, to them gave He power to become the sons of God, even to them that believe on His Name" (John 1:12, KJV).

Emily, the timid mother-to-be, eventually received the gift of salvation. Three months before her baby was born, she became a child of God. He changed her inwardly, and it showed on her face. Her blue eyes shone as she said, "Knowing God loves me wipes away my thoughts that I'm a useless nobody. I feel free because I know He cares about me and wants me, even though I'm not perfect."

A woman from the church studied the Bible with Emily each week and a friendship developed. This woman not only taught Emily about God, but she also showed her how to be a better woman, wife, and mother — even a decent cook. This fundamental dynamic of a woman's life, her relationship with Christ, released Emily from fear. Her new security enabled hidden strengths to surface, and she became a different woman.

Jesus Gives Me A New Image

As we follow Christ our self-esteem improves. The worldly emphasis on life's basic "essentials" — a prestigious family or physical attractiveness — are overridden by our attachment to Him. We focus more on how we live and how we love than on how we look. We look for ways we can best use our talents for Him rather than for ourselves.

As you study the life of Christ, you will see in Him a dynamic role model. You'll learn that His earthly heritage and appearance were lowly and unappealing, but He was secure. He knew who He was in His relationship with the Father: "He grew up before him like a tender shoot, and like a root out of the dry ground. He had no beauty or majesty to attract us to Him, nothing in His appearance that we should desire Him. He was despised and rejected by men, a man of sorrows, and familiar with suffering. Like one from whom men hide their faces He was despised, and we esteemed Him not" (Isaiah 53:2,3).

When you become God's child, you put on a new self (Colossians 3:10). God transforms your inner being. The new self is identified with Christ and esteemed by God rather than man. In Him, you are complete in your self-image. A woman created in the image of God, distinct in her family heritage, unique in her looks, personality and abilities, with her inner being spiritually transformed, is a whole person.

On days when I feel insignificant, I think about this new image, the specialness of the personal relationship I now have with Christ. If I ever catch my reflection in a mirror and see a questioning woman wondering, *Who am I?* I respond, *I am a woman, unique in the universe, with personal worth, because I am loved by God and complete in Christ.*

This dynamic relationship with Christ, accompanied by His voice saying, *"You belong to me,"* makes a woman feel secure. It frees her to mature, to discover her creative potential, and to explore ways to use it.

3
How Can I Grow?

*Cooperating with God
is the dynamic for growing in maturity*

The truth settled slowly in my mind: We were really moving from the Midwest to the deep South. Thoughts of leaving stirred up waves of nostalgia, buffeting my emotions. One moment I was laughing over the memory of good times and the next I was bursting into tears over the same memory. In quieter moments a nagging question bothered me: Could I adjust to such a change? My patterns of life had become so intertwined with the rhythm of the changing seasons that I could predict exactly what I would do and how I would feel from week to week.

I was comfortable with this flow of life. I was attached to this part of the country. The friendly town was our home. It was where our three children were born, raised and rooted in relationships and experiences. Leaving the familiar faces of even the bank teller and clerks troubled me. Considering my dearest friends, I wondered, *How can I be separated from people I feel so close to — those with whom I've shared a lifetime?*

The people at church had been my family for the twenty-seven years my husband had been the pastor and I felt a strong bond with them. We had grown up together, teaching each other lessons in loving and forgiving.

Facing New Situations

"You need to be brave." This was the phrase my mother often used when I was faced with a new situation, or when anything was going to hurt, like having my tonsils removed. I now needed a good dose of that distinctive quality of maturity — bravery.

Reflecting on past changes helped me to see the value of being brave and reminded me of how I could muster strength. One incident, for example, stood out in my mind. I thought a lot about Beverly, a childhood friend whose spirit was as adventuresome as her hair was red. Unbound by rules, she freely investigated her world and I went along for the ride. Daily I went down the alley behind our house to meet her at her front door so we could walk to school together. We did everything together — whispered to each other in class, walked the eight blocks home after school, changed to play clothes and climbed trees in our back-yard.

I remember one Friday when Mother said I could sleep overnight at Beverly's house. I would have to abide by our family rule: "Don't call home and ask me to come and get you. Be brave; you can make it through the night."

I remember how surprised I was to hear Beverly talk back to her mother when she threatened to spank Beverly with a wooden spoon. I felt confused when there was no set bedtime, when we could eat whatever we wanted, whenever we wanted. My uneasiness grew to discomfort by the time Beverly and I curled up in bed. Neither red hair nor adventure impressed me late that night in Beverly's strange bedroom. I wanted to be home in my own bed, asleep by my older sister.

As I lay in bed, in my mind's eye I could see my mother sitting in her chair in the living room, embroidering and talking to my father. I could see her soft brown eyes and the speck of a mole on her right cheek, and I could hear her voice saying, "Be brave; you can make it through the night." That image helped me finally to fall asleep in that unfamiliar situation.

What gives you courage? Is it someone's encouraging voice or a pleasant memory? Emotional maturity doesn't just happen naturally like physical growth; it doesn't follow a set pattern. It evolves from accumulating and blending many positive experiences and surviving negative ones. From each new situation, we learn lessons about our needs and how to survive. Adapting to an overnight visit like I did at Beverly's house is an example of those types of experiences that contribute to the maturing process.

Adjusting to New Relationships

Growing in maturity not only involves courageously adapting to a new setting, but it also involves developing adaptability in relationships. Grandmas, sisters and friends provide us with opportunities to interact with others and, in turn, to learn about ourselves. From these early interpersonal relationships we also learn how to relate to different personalities. Each experience in relating and adapting prepares us for that deep relationship with one significant person in the union of marriage.

If you're married, you can recall how that relationship began. I was a teenager at a Christian camp when I saw the man of my dreams materialize before my eyes. He looked exactly like the one I had sketched in my mind from the time I was ten. And he was real, with beautiful, penetrating eyes that seemed to look right into my heart.

All week, I watched him talk with people, throw a football and walk on the beach. I even sat at a table where I could see him at mealtime and noticed how he ate and the way he laughed.

Toward the end of the week, he asked me to sit with him in church. Afterward we drank milkshakes and walked the path to the Lake Michigan beach. We talked in the moonlight and held hands on the way back to the cabin. It was hard to fall asleep that night because I kept thinking of his eyes, wondering if he noticed how fast my heart beat and how attracted I was to him.

Many letters and two years of college later, he surprised me. Just at sunset in the roughed-in entrance to the nursery of the church under construction (a church he would later co-pastor with his father), Dave asked me to marry him. I was dazed because I was still a student. Yet I was confident that saying yes was the best decision I would ever make. That August we honeymooned at the camp where we had met. Our romance had come full circle.

But our idyllic relationship developed a strain, and my romantic feelings wavered the first time we disagreed. We struggled with a difference in sleeping patterns. David's metabolic clock was set for the late night hours and mine was for the morning. Both of us would have to make some adjustments. And it took a long time to work through these "timely" differences.

Adapting To New Responsibilities

The single best measuring stick of maturity is the extent of one's ability to adapt. I naively thought I measured up. I had argued with and learned to adapt to two sisters at home and a roommate in college. But resolving an area of difference with my husband was new and more serious. We were romantic marriage partners and I didn't want to destroy our closeness. I had much to learn.

"To make fit as for a new use or situation," is the dictionary definition of *adapt.* In marriage the goal is to "make fit" for the partner — to strive for compatibility. This is a tough assignment, to be like elastic. We're adaptable if we easily stretch to try new ideas or changes and recover quickly to a healthy emotional state. Learning to put aside selfishness and share our beds with our husbands calls for lifelong flexibility.

No sooner do we make changes in one area of marriage than need for another adjustment confronts us as new responsibilities are assumed. Coping with the pressure to adjust may seem like dodging balls which are shooting rapid-fire from the lever of a pin-ball machine. No wonder we feel insecure when faced with a variety of new demands.

I was overwhelmed when Dave and I moved from our secure little college apartment to his home town. We had lived unto ourselves the first nine months of marriage and suddenly many new people entered our lives. His family, friends and church members were new to me, as were his long days away from home. He eagerly launched into co-pastoring the church with his father. The unknowns of being a pastor's wife made me feel unsure of myself. I'd had no previous experience with people watching every detail of my life and openly expressing their opinions about me.

Then I began having babies — two girls thirteen months apart. Caring for our home and the babies were responsibilities that took more physical and emotional energy than I had counted on. Changing diapers, preparing formula, cleaning the high-chair tray and scrubbing the floor from spills were such drudgery. I never seemed to have time for myself. Many days I felt like I had shortly before I fell asleep at Beverly's house. I wanted to go home. I wanted to put our two babies aside for awhile. I wanted to go back and play house like I had done during the early months of our marriage.

Don't you sometimes long to be carefree again? I think we all feel like quitting or returning to childhood days at times, but, "It's too soon to quit." That was a phrase Dr. V. Raymond Edman had quoted often to us students when he was president of Wheaton College, and I had repeated it to myself during exams. Years later I repeated it to myself during long nights of feeding our babies.

A mature woman needs a stick-to-it-iveness in tending to her responsibilities. Persistence includes enduring unpleasantness on many levels, and hardships of varying degrees. It's a mental attitude. At needy times it surfaces and forcefully dictates to the mind and body, "Press on," or it creeps into the mind with a soft whisper, "It's too soon to quit."

The lines of the Scottish ballad Ronald Reagan quoted in his 1976 election concession speech strongly evoke a stay-with-it spirit: "Lay me down and bleed a while. Though I am wounded, I am not slain...I shall rise and fight again." This captures the attitude of triumphant determination.

Whether caring for her family, tending to her home, or using her talents and gifts, a mature woman stays with it in carrying out her tasks. She is persistent.

Recognizing My Real Needs

Human effort and persistence can get us through many routine days of mothering and working hard at a profession. But do you yearn for something more? I did. I wanted to hum with satisfaction as I went through each day. Rather than generating courage and persistence from raw determination, I desired help from within — from my spirit.

One day in desperation I knelt by my bed, put my face in the familiar quilt and begged God, "Forgive me for neglecting what I need the most. Help; I need You."

I realize that my situation wasn't the desperate kind that many women face. Nonetheless I was lonely and I felt isolated and in need of inner strength. That incident marked the beginning of my coming to God regularly and developing an ongoing relationship with Him.

As a result, He put a desire in my heart to study His Word and I began growing in spiritual knowledge. His Word nourished the core of my being; it flowed into my thoughts, my feelings and, in turn, renewed my body. I found this refreshing.

My responsibilities stayed the same, but there was a change in the inner me — new peace, joy, purpose. I began to focus outside myself, like I did at Beverly's house when I wanted to go home. Only this time, I mentally set my eyes on the person of Jesus Christ instead of on my mother's face.

Studying His Word was like looking into a mirror. His words reminded me that I belonged to Him and that He was available to help me make it through each night, and through life. These new insights changed my perspective on coping with daily struggles. My renewed relationship with Christ brought the concept of maturity into sharper focus. Without the spiritual dynamic, our bravery, adaptability and persistence efforts are inadequate human resources.

We are like clouds without rain when we try to be mature without Christ. God puts within us a new capacity for spiritual energy which undergirds and strengthens our striving for maturity. He enables us to attain the various dimensions of maturity. The dynamic relationship we have with Christ gives us courage. His power within gives us confidence and enables us to be brave. The apostle Paul writes: "I pray also that the eyes of your heart may be enlightened in order to know...his incomparably great power for us who believe" (Ephesians 1:18,19).

Possessing Spiritual Vitality

The vitalizing force or dynamic of Christian maturity is unleashed when we cooperate with God. Our participation involves a two step process: knowing God's Word, and yielding to that knowledge. In our relationship with God, His agent, the Holy Spirit, convinces us to act on the knowledge of His Word. The mature Christian yields to the Holy Spirit, learning to recognize His voice. We talk to God in prayer, He talks to us through His Word. In this team effort, God produces the fruit of the Spirit in the inner person: love, joy, peace, patience, kindness, goodness, faithfulness, gentleness and self-control (Galatians 5:22,23).

Reading, memorizing and meditating on the Bible constitute our primary tasks. God uses these activities to teach us truth and to show us how to apply it to our lives. His words and thoughts are powerful, creating healthy attitudes which in turn affect our feelings and even our bodies.

Yielding to what God wants us to do is a more difficult task because it involves our will. Directions from the Bible seem to run directly counter to what we feel like doing at times. For example, who wants to praise God when life is dull, difficult or uncomfortable? Yet we read: "Through Jesus, therefore, let us continually offer to God a sacrifice of praise — the fruit of lips that confess his name" (Hebrews 13:15).

When we feel the routine of life is closing in on us or we're carrying a responsibility which feels burdensome, God's Word says to praise Him. Praising Him in tough times as well as in good times is a sign we're yielding to God's direction. Our thoughts and complaints about insurmountable tasks or plain boredom need to be translated to praise for who He is and what He will do for us in the inner person.

Author Alexander Solzhenitsyn, who spent eight years in Stalin's labor camp, said:

> Live with a steady superiority over life — don't be afraid of misfortune, and do not yearn after happiness; it is, after all, the same: The bitter doesn't last forever, and the sweet never fills the cup to overflowing....It is enough if you don't freeze in the cold and if thirst and hunger don't claw at your insides. If your back isn't broken, if your feet can walk, if both arms can bend, if both eyes can see, both ears hear.[1]

Focusing outside ourselves on God and praising Him refreshes our mind, renews our spirit and pleases Him. When we yield to Him, He strengthens us, empowers us, and produces within us an abundance of love, joy, peace and all spiritual fruit.

The dynamic of this cooperative relationship with God is visible when a woman radiates a composed, pleasant manner as she fulfills her daily responsibilities. Calmness as she faces her tasks, even as the frustrations mount, reflects her yieldedness to the Holy Spirit. She's free from agitation when she's up against difficulty because she trusts God to help her with each situation.

I observed this attitude in one of the nurses who cared for me when I was in the hospital. While some of the nurses were rough and spoke loudly, complaining and blaming others, this nurse worked in a refreshingly quiet way, bearing a smile and a gentle touch. Early one morning I asked her about her pleasantness. "I have four young children at home," she said softly.

"Three of them are in school, in kindergarten through third grade. The fourth is handicapped. We need money from my income to pay for his extra needs. Otherwise, I wouldn't be here. Before I put my feet on the floor in the morning I praise God. I begin by thanking Him for each of our children and committing myself and the events of the day to Him. As I work here in the hospital, I pray for each patient as I go from room to room. I believe I'm God's agent of loving care while I'm here."

Obeying Biblical Commands

In what areas of your life do you struggle to obey Him? Is it difficult for you to praise God continually? Can you easily adapt to others? More important, will you adapt to your husband so God can build oneness in your relationship? Peter encourages all women to demonstrate this yieldedness, but especially women married to unbelievers: "In the same spirit you married women should adapt yourselves to your husbands, so that even if they do not obey the Word of God, they may be won to God without any word being spoken" (1 Peter 3:1, J.B. Phillips).

It was some years ago when Laura first called me. She was in tears and deeply concerned about her marriage. I didn't know her at the time and I couldn't see her, but in my mind's eye I visualized a woman with a perfectly styled hairdo. She'd be immaculately dressed. I could almost smell her delicate perfume. I had previously met her husband, an adventurous outdoors man. Their opposite lifestyles and tastes seemed to be behind all the trouble.

She said, "My husband and I are growing apart. We disagree about his motorcycling. He wants me to ride on the back of his bike and take weekend trips with him. First of all, that means I would miss church, and riding on the motorcycle would mean I would need to put a helmet over my hair and wear slacks — neither of which I like. How can I look attractive and feel like a lady in clothes like that? I'd get filthy riding in the open air all day. Even worse is the thought of associating with his biking buddies who would accompany us."

The wall of bad feelings that had grown up between her and her husband demanded quick action or the barrier would harden until it was permanent. She took 1 Peter 3 to heart and decided to do what would make her non-Christian husband happy. First she prayed and told God she was willing to adapt to the desires of her husband. Then, drawing on His strength, she set aside her pride and self-will and consciously submitted herself to her husband, bravely mounting his motorcycle.

Each Saturday and Sunday that spring she rode behind her husband — through rain and sunshine, up and down steep winding roads and narrow flat ones in various parts of Ohio. Along with other cyclists they stopped in small country towns for lunch and dinner, often eating from their own picnic basket — fried chicken and special baked treats she had prepared.

One night she followed her husband into a damp, musty-smelling, empty trailer where they spent the night along with several other couples. As she lay in her sleeping bag by her husband, she suddenly felt his arm around her. As she relaxed in his warm embrace, she heard the words of love and appreciation she had so desperately longed for. Her silent prayer was, *Oh, God, I don't believe I'm here, but thank You, I am.*

That summer, when they were home on Sundays, her husband began attending her church and seeking out other people like his wife as friends because he enjoyed their company. By the time leaves were on the ground and the air was too cold to motorcycle, her husband was attending church regularly. Near Thanksgiving he yielded his life to Jesus Christ. His response had evolved out of the attractive qualities reflected in his wife. God used her actions to change his life and their relationship. Their marriage entered a new phase of togetherness. She experienced the reward of seeing God's promise.

Years later, a rare disease shot pain through her husband's nervous system. She cared for his body and comforted him. When her beloved husband died in her arms, she praised God through her tears for the life they had shared together and for directing her to the principle of adaptability. She would need it to face the future without her mate.

Being Faithful In Tough Times

Our faith is tested when we experience difficulties. Relationship problems, loss of a loved one or financial setbacks are not easy. Rather than blaming and forsaking God during hard times, we can mature in our faith if we persevere.

James expresses the process like this: "The testing of your faith develops perseverance. Perseverance must finish its work so that you may be mature and complete, not lacking anything" (James 1:3,4).

Each of us experiences difficulties in various forms. Our trials can be like street lights directing us to God. Tough times can be a stimulus, nudging us to pray and teaching us a healthy dependence on Him. The reward for our faithfulness in yielding to Him is what happens deep down inside. Comfort from the Holy Spirit flows over our spirit into our mind, with a calming effect.

A mature woman who is sustained by the Holy Spirit is identified by this sweet spirit. It increases as the difficulty intensifies, bearing witness that God is at work. You'll want to get in the habit of yielding to the Spirit's conviction. Following His directions will produce a fully mature woman. "And God...after you have suffered a little while, will himself restore you and make you strong, firm and steadfast" (1 Peter 5:10).

Which life passage are you going through? Take time to identify some current opportunities for growth going on in your life. Have you tried to keep a journal? You can at least jot down a few "areas of concern" in the flyleaf of your Bible. Keep track of your progress. It'll be an encouragement to you. Each difficulty is an opportunity to step out in faith and grow in dynamic cooperation with God. Each time we are stretched, a new lesson prepares us for who we are and where we are today in maturity.

My accumulated life experiences in being brave, adapting and persevering helped me in our move from the Midwest to the South, but it took more than that; leaving the warmth of friendships and the oneness with the mood of the seasons was possible only because I determined to cooperate with God. I began by memorizing and hanging my heart on the words God gave Joshua: "Be strong and courageous. Do not be terrified; do not be discouraged, for the LORD your God will be with you wherever you go" (Joshua 1:9).

Moving day was a gloomy morning in early autumn. The movers loaded the truck, carrying each item through a light drizzle. By late afternoon, the truck had pulled away with our possessions and Dave and I walked through the empty rooms of the home we had lived in with our three children. Dozens of memories moved rapidly through my mind, triggering tears to mirror the wet outdoors.

When we had examined the last room, we knelt on the bare floor and lifted our hearts to the one who had blessed us with those memories. As we yielded and entrusted our unknown future to Him, He did His work in us and steadied our hearts and minds and renewed our courage. Like a streak of sunlight through the gloom came the words: "He is with you wherever you go."

Today this verse is framed and hangs on my wall in our new home in Florida. Whenever I glance at it, my inner being fills with praise and a smile breaks out. I have certainly experienced its truth. Cooperating with God *is* dynamic.

Looking closer at the promise in Joshua, another part of the verse jumps out at me: "Do not be terrified; do not be discouraged." This is a reminder of another inner dynamic — learning to control the anxiety which hinders my maturity in Christ.

4
Why Can't I Stop Worrying?

*Spending time with Jesus
is the dynamic for controlling anxiety*

Have you ever experienced the overwhelming grip of anxiety? Memories of how it gripped me are still vivid. One night our bedroom clock showed 1 A.M. My body was tired, but I had an awful feeling that kept me from falling asleep. My husband had commented casually that he was going to bring a well-known evangelist home for dinner sometime while he was a guest at our church. I don't know how I responded, but I remember the strange sensation in my stomach.

The evangelist was a dignified gentleman. I just *knew* he had been treated to every sort of exquisite cuisine in America. It seemed like such a big order: Plan a special menu; clean the house; make sure our two lively girls would be in bed; see to it that I looked presentable for such a noted guest. I lay awake a long time that night. I imagined the evangelist stumbling over a misplaced toy as he entered our small house. I visualized him frowning in disgust after touching a tabletop sticky from a misplaced popsicle stick. But the nagging questions that really haunted me were: What was good enough for such a great man to eat? Could I cook it to his satisfaction? What if everything went wrong and he told people across the country what a foolish wife Pastor Burnham had?

Why do we dwell on such thoughts and become so fearful? I realize now that I had all the symptoms of "anxiety disease": feelings of being threatened, of uneasiness, and of self-doubt. In the mind of an anxious person, the list of dreadful thoughts is endless. Plans to entertain the evangelist had stirred up uneasy feelings and self-doubt concerning the house, food, children, my appearance and even my husband's reputation. Looking back on the situation, I recognize the pattern of worry. It robbed me of time, energy and an enjoyable evening.

Tracing my anxious feelings to their source led me to three root causes First, my self-esteem was threatened by doubts about my appearance and adequacy. Second, my personal welfare was threatened by doubts about the future and concern for material things. Third, my well-being was threatened by unresolved conflicts.

How Do I Look?

How many of us women wrap our self-worth in our appearance? Aren't we led to believe that if we look good enough we will feel secure? No wonder we fear the loss of self-respect and close relationships when we think of gaining weight or aging. Wrinkles, gray hair and fat are to be avoided at all cost. Who could love those qualities? Withered, worn and large is how we see ourselves in later life — discarded by a world that honors youth, beauty and, above all, a slim figure.

I recall a fashionably dressed woman who came to me one day. Nervously she began describing her relationship with her husband. He was drinking too much and coming home late. She felt desperate. She knew she was losing the man she loved. In her mind, there could be no reason for this except that her body was changing due to age. Her hands and voice trembled. She asserted that the only way to secure his love again was to work on her appearance. She felt she had to try to look sexier.

What's going on inside health spas, boutiques and beauty salons? They're simply making rigorous efforts to improve and maintain our physical appearance. Our emotional need to be valuable launches us toward efforts to make ourselves look good. This *temporarily* quiets our fears.

How Am I Doing?

As soon as we think we've found a cure for one fear, the anxiety disease breaks out somewhere else. We become victims of other anxieties. Is my work good enough? Is the house clean enough? Are the children nice enough? Am I assertive, kind, social, charitable enough? And with so many demands, how can I find enough time to get everything done?

We desire expressions of approval for what we do. As little girls, we wanted to do well to please our mothers. At each developing age we listen for a special voice. The teacher, coach, employer or admired peer becomes a significant *other* from whom we need to hear approval. They affirm us, and we feel we're good enough.

In time, we develop our own rating scale. This tends to become our primary standard of performance. When we don't successfully measure up to our predetermined standard (which is perfection on some women's scales), we *feel* unacceptable. This struggle with performance is often an open door to anxiety.

The most damaging anxiety attack is subtle. It's the syndrome of doubting our spiritual worth. Before we trust Christ, we fear: Am I good enough to become a Christian? After we take the plunge, doubts may persist. Then we start asking something like, Am I a good enough Christian? Spiritual insecurity creeps into our minds.

Am I Doing Enough?

Joyce was a woman in her thirties who sold real estate. She described her situation as impossible. She felt constant pressure from her workload and her compulsion to do so many things. She was overcome with anxiety. Many inner selves tugged for her attention. One self called out, "Sell enough houses and you'll be somebody." Other responsible selves cried out with equal appeal, "Give time to your family; develop your singing voice; volunteer time to the school and community." Her tense body leaned forward as she asked, "How much is enough?"

Women tend to accept endless demands. By doing so we hope to reduce the anxiety of the deeply-rooted question, How can I, or my husband, or anybody, love and accept me if I'm not doing more and trying to do it better? Like Joyce, we come to a crisis point. We find ourselves threatened, uncertain.

What's Going To Happen To Me?

Who hasn't worried about what the future will bring and whether or not she'll have enough money to live on? Such thoughts are closely tied to fears concerning personal survival and welfare. Our overly active minds periodically put our bodies through their paces and take anxious accounts of creaks and wheezes. The prospect of a cancerous lump signals anxiety to some degree in every woman. For the highly anxious woman it's a prophecy of doom. Real or imagined aches and pains, the chances of having an accident or being the victim of a crime — in short, anything that could harm the body — weigh heavily with the anxious person. She is really preparing herself for the ultimate: death.

Recently, I chauffeured a 50-year-old woman from the bus depot to her mother's funeral. On the way to the home, Clara talked incessantly about the world's perils. "Flying in airplanes is risky; that's why I took the bus," she said, shaking her head from side to side. I also learned that urban crime had scared her into buying a country house.

The one thing she wouldn't talk about was her mother and the circumstances of her death. But as we arrived at the funeral home she started to cry and sobbed uncontrollably as she viewed the body. She repeatedly said, "It's so awful; I can't stand it." Her own body began to shake and friends helped her to a chair. Her legs had turned to rubber and she was filled with such emotion she began to hyperventilate; then she passed out. The reality of death was too hard for her to face.

Like Clara, you may try to hide your deepest anxieties. We cry when we experience the loss of someone we love, but our responses may be symptomatic of something more than grief. Mixed with it is a measure of our own fear: What will become of me?

What Should I Do?

Another basic cause of anxiety is conflict revolving around decision-making. What will I serve the well-known evangelist? Fried chicken, ham, roast beef? No, they're too common. How about Italian or Mexican? No, too spicy, too hot. Why not the extra turkey in the freezer? Maybe.

Competing alternatives wage war in any decision-making process — if not our menu, then which dresses, cars or houses to buy? Which job to take? Which is worse — aches and pains we have now or the pain that would follow surgery? Once a decision is made, anxiety subsides. But then another anxiety of self-doubt nags: Was the decision right, or did I make a mistake?

Why Can't I Stop Worrying?

Anxiety can result also from a conflict repressed or buried deep in the subconscious. Tracing uneasy feelings to their source is difficult. It takes time. Intense emotional experiences can lie deeply buried in your unconscious, unresolved. Anxiety is triggered when the experience and the accompanying feeling move toward conscious awareness. It's a perpetual cycle.

Evelyn, a large, strong-looking woman in her early forties, lived a wild life. In a conscious effort to quiet her gnawing anxiety, she was drinking too much, driving recklessly and behaving in ways she wouldn't normally condone. She sputtered out a few words to me, attempting to describe her problem: "When I try to pray, I become so anxious I'm miserable. The same troublesome feelings are aroused when I go to church or participate in religious activities. I've discontinued all my religious involvement, but I don't like the way I'm living. I feel ashamed. On the average Friday night, I get on my motorcycle, ride it to a bar and drink myself into oblivion."

After exploring many possibilities for her anxiety, we talked about her father's death. Her reaction when he died lent a clue to her behavior. She said, "I didn't cry or talk about my grief because I, the oldest child, wanted to be strong for my younger brothers and sisters and my mother." She considered this stoic response virtuous. Consequently she denied her trauma and repressed her sorrow.

In counseling sessions Evelyn shared bits and pieces of information until the whole story was told. Finally, she talked about her love for her father. She had felt hurt and angry over his death. She admitted, "I felt closer to him than to any other person because I was so like him in so many ways and he was so good to me." Apologetically she confessed, "I guess I secretly blamed God for taking my father away. I was only twelve years old and too young to understand."

Is it any wonder she choked up and was overwhelmed with anxiety when she tried to pray? How can you trust the one you're angry with?

Facing her heart-breaking trauma and probing it, and understanding death's tie to sin rather than to God, resolved her anxiety. Twenty-five years after her father's death, this woman permitted herself to grieve. She experienced God's comfort. She experienced freedom to worship and serve Him.

Anxiety is a tormenter. In its strongest form, it's an apprehension that grabs hold of the mind. It triggers hidden feelings and invades inner crannies. Like a broken record, the negative message is heard over and over in the mind. *Something bad is going to happen to me; I don't know exactly what, but I must be ready for it.*

Can you identify an experience that causes you to worry? You usually can trace your uneasy feelings to one of three basic sources: a threat to self-esteem, concern for the future, or unresolved conflicts. Understanding the source of your anxiety is a step toward controlling this unruly foe. As you recognize the negative consequences of anxiety in your life, do you wonder, What's the use of worrying anyway?

Can I Break The Worry Cycle?

God gave us the capacity to be concerned about protecting our physical well-being. In one sense, anxiety is the kick that gets us out of bed in the morning to accomplish our tasks. When our bodies tell us we want sleep, our mind, stirring with concern, says, *You can't sleep; you have work to do.* The Bible teaches believers how anxiety (translated "care") can work in a healthy way. Scripture encourages us to care (be anxious) for others and not to care only for ourselves (1 Corinthians 12:25; Philippians 2:20).

Anxiety also has the potential to dominate our lives. The Bible says, "An anxious heart weighs a man down" (Proverbs 12:25). Is it any wonder that an anxious person feels tired all the time? Energy meant for working and enjoying life is wasted by worry. Constantly attending to emotional issues which won't lie still saps physical strength. Responding to the anxiety alarm, our bodies work hard — muscles straining, pulse racing, stomach tightening. With our system at high speed, our mind is less efficient, and our concentration is hindered by fearful thoughts.

Worrying doesn't enhance our appearance either. Anxiety accelerates the aging process, etching its footprints in our faces. Under the weight of anxiety's demands, our dispositions also are affected. Irritability and nervousness infect the atmosphere, touching all who come into contact with us.

Our children are quick to mimic our examples. They learn to react to the stresses of life by adopting the same anxious patterns they see us live out. Does your child see you respond positively when things seem to be building up?

The story of Mary and Martha, in whose home Jesus spent many pleasant hours, provides the backdrop for Jesus' teaching on how to overcome worry. Luke 10:38-42 describes Martha as an anxious woman. Along with her sister Mary and her brother Lazarus, Martha was entertaining Jesus, and most likely His disciples, for dinner. This was a relaxing time for Jesus. His friends' home was a refreshing retreat from Jerusalem's bustling marketplace and the demanding crowds.

On this occasion, Martha welcomed Jesus and returned to the kitchen for final dinner preparations. We can imagine that she was tired. She had already worked hard, but she began to worry about whether or not Jesus would appreciate her efforts. As she hurried to finish the details, she glanced into the breezy courtyard from her heated kitchen and saw Mary. She felt Mary had taken advantage of her. Putting aside graciousness, she lashed out at Jesus, saying, "Lord, don't You care that my sister has left me to do the work by myself? Tell her to help me."

Jesus didn't answer the question directly. Instead He went to the heart of the issue and said, "Martha, Martha, you are worried and upset about many things." Martha — not Mary — had the problem. Mary became a target of Martha's anxiety, but Mary's not working wasn't the issue — the issue was worry.

Jesus had come to the home in Bethany to be refreshed, "but Martha was distracted by all the preparations that had to be made." Her self-esteem was threatened. She inwardly questioned her abilities: *Is the food good enough to maintain my reputation as an outstanding cook?* Her anxiety and uneasiness affected everyone there, disrupting the atmosphere of rest.

What Did Mary Choose?

Martha was so involved in her work and in attending to her own emotional needs that she missed the heart of the matter. Mary chose the better part. She simply "sat at Jesus' feet listening to what He said." Martha bypassed that quiet time with Jesus. It would have renewed her strength — He was available to minister to her. He wanted to deliver her from worry and trouble, but she lost perspective. Overly tired, keyed up by high anxiety, she resorted to her only human respite: to blame Mary.

Arranging time daily to be with God calms the woman who worries. As He fills the needs of her soul, earthly cares diminish. Assured of His care and her worth to Him, her tasks become easier. Jesus offered Martha security, not in a magical way, but by revealing to her the basis of security: a rich, eternal relationship with Himself.

Martha eventually learned this truth. Later, at the funeral of her brother, she professed that Jesus was the Son of God and that He held the power of life and death. Believing in Him gave her the ultimate security of eternal life (John 11:21-27). As she focused her mind on the dynamic of knowing Christ, her ongoing experience was serene rather than anxious. Her value as a person wasn't determined by her reputation for hospitality. It was affirmed by Jesus' love and acceptance.

Trusting in Christ's care can shield us from every threat. But we must step under His faithful protection like my friend Beth did. Nobody would have suspected she was an alcoholic. She kept her house in order and pursued a career, but she used alcohol to deaden her anxiety. She feared not being able to make ends meet, and she worried constantly about dying. At first, alcohol dulled her senses. It quieted her fearful thoughts through the night. But soon she found herself dependent on it.

Beth's worries were compounded by the fear that her family and friends would find out. In her frightened condition she sought God. Timidly, she began attending a Bible study. After several months, she trusted God's promise of forgiveness. She relinquished her unhealthy dependence on alcohol and put her faith in Christ. He gave her assurance of both eternal life and daily care.

My friend chose to listen to the words of Jesus. This enabled her to resolve the anxieties plaguing her life. Amazingly, we can *know* intellectually that we have eternal life. We *know* we have power to be fearless as we face death. Yet as Christians, we still continue to worry. Spending time with Jesus can change that. It did for Mary. And Beth.

How Will Spending Time With God Help Me?

By eight o'clock each morning I'm in a quiet part of our house with a cup of coffee, my Bible, a pen and a notebook. I read the Bible and work on a specific lesson. Then I do some memorizing and meditating. After I spend time with Jesus, I'm reminded of His friendship and how much He cares for me. I begin each day with genuine security.

Along with reading the Bible, I talk with God more openly than I talk with any other friend. During my prayer time I confess any sins which the Word of God has brought to light. This confession time eliminates the worry that my sin will separate me from Jesus. Then I share with Him all my cares and the desires of my heart, remembering His command, "Cast all your anxiety on Him because He cares for you" (1 Peter 5:7).

While it's still quiet and I'm in His presence, I take a few minutes to think about solutions to conflicts which would otherwise cause me to worry. I think about such questions as, Which do I need more, to buy a new dress or to have the carpet cleaned? Should I call Jon (our son in college) and offer my opinion or let him figure it out by himself? Which one of the Christian service opportunities should I get involved in?

At times, when I remain undecided about choices, I write down each consideration and place them in my Bible. Then I pray over them, asking God to give me insight either from His Word or through clear thinking. The Bible promises: "For God hath not given us the spirit of fear, but of power, and of love, and of a sound mind" (2 Timothy 1:7, King James Version).

When I'm tempted to worry, I remind myself that I have an appointed time for dealing with these pressing matters. Then I reflect on a verse from the Bible or a helpful thought borrowed from my quiet time lessons.

The following are some verses drawn from those solitary hours. These have proven to be lifesavers for me, lifting me out of anxiety. You can refer to these verses daily. In times of crisis, you may find them especially helpful.

MY RESPONSIBILITY	GOD'S REWARD
Spend time daily with God in Bible reading, prayer and meditation.	"You will keep in perfect peace him whose mind is steadfast because he trusts in you" (Isaiah 26:3).
	"In everything . . . present your request to God. And the peace of God . . . will guard your hearts and your minds in Christ Jesus" Philippians 4:6,7).
	"Trust in the Lord and do good . . . . Delight yourself in the Lord and he will give you the desires of your heart." (Psalm 37:3,4).
By choice, exchange a fearful thought for one of	"[Nothing] will be able to separate us from the love

God's promises.

of God that is in Christ
Jesus our Lord"
(Romans 8:39).

"My peace I give you
(John 14:27).

"Cast all your anxiety
on him because he cares
for you" (1 Peter 5:7).

"And my God will meet all
your needs . . ."
(Philippians 4:19).

Plan carefully; set realistic
standards.

"God will take care of your
tomorrow too. Live one
day at a time" (Matthew
6:34, The Living Bible).

THREATS

PROMISES

Self-esteem threatened by
doubts concerning
appearance.

"She is clothed with
strength and dignity . . . .
Beauty is fleeting; but a
woman who fears the Lord
is to be praised" (Proverbs
31:25-30).

Self-esteem threatened by
doubts of adequacy.

"Well done, good and
faithful servant!"
(Matthew 25:21).

Personal welfare threat-
ened by doubts of the
future.

"So don't be anxious about
tomorrow. God will take
care of your tomorrow too.
Live one day at a time"
(Matthew 6:34).

| Personal welfare threatened by death. | "You may know that you have eternal life" (1 John 5:13). |
| Well being threatened by unresolved conflicts. | "Be still before the Lord and wait patiently for him" (Psalm 37:7). |

God's Word is dynamic. It is living, powerful and true. These promises will begin to permeate your consciousness, your inner being. No other weapon can so utterly destroy anxiety's stronghold and set you free to be at peace with yourself. You'll find it *is* possible to control anxiety.

Do you long for the joy of ongoing spiritual fellowship? But do you find that something comes between you and God whenever you enter His presence? What can you do if darkness broods over your spirit, holding you back from Him?

5
What Can I Do About My Mood Swings?

Knowing Jesus understands
is the dynamic for dispelling depression

It was a shock. The first time I saw patients in the State Mental Health Center was an oppressive experience. It stabbed my heart and aroused queasy feelings in my stomach.

I mechanically followed the nurse through the Center. We came upon a woman bent forward on a straight-backed chair, her hands covering her eyes. When she finally lifted her head to answer the doctor's questions, strands of unwashed hair parted, revealing a pallid face. Dark circles under red and swollen eyes were further evidence of extreme trauma. She said only a few words, then returned to her former posture, crying until her already weakened body convulsed with sobs.

I had read textbook descriptions of depression. I had experienced moments of mild forms of it myself. But nothing had prepared me for the intensity of depression I saw that day. Later I learned that even the most depressed patients usually get better. As the nurse led me away from the emergency area, we entered another ward. There I saw patients who had started coming out of their severe depression.

The mood of the patients in this area was clearly improved from the overwhelming despair of the woman in the Emergency Room. The nurse later told me that that patient hadn't eaten or slept for several days before she was admitted. However, the severe darkness of the depressed patients in this lounge had begun to lift once they started regular treatment. No one laughed or smiled here yet, but no one cried either. Their mood could best be described as a gloom somewhere between death and life — inactivity basically, except for a shuffling movement now and then. Rather than walking, which involved too much effort, they would push and slide their feet.

As a final step before release, patients were transferred to a separate unit on an outpatient basis. I found that the atmosphere in that ward encouraged activity, the mood was more upbeat and the faces looked brighter. As I left, I reflected on the note of hope inherent in the progress I had seen. In my heart, I clung to the promises of recovery I had witnessed that day.

Accept Need For Renewal

Depressed people can take courage from the fact that they are capable of recovery, but for many, depression will continue to be their enemy. Like any disease, it attacks a weak, vulnerable spot. A deeply emotional man, the psalmist David was vulnerable to depression. In one dark hour he prayed: "Save me, O God, for the waters have come up to my neck. I sink in the miry depths, where there is no foothold. I have come into the deep waters; the floods engulf me. I am worn out calling for help; my throat is parched. My eyes fail, looking for my God" (Psalm 69:1-3). The Bible portrays David, and others like him, in their humanity.

Some contemporary Christians are willing, in a Christ-like attitude of love and truth, to open the door of their lives and permit others to see in and learn from their struggles with depression. Cynthia Swindoll, executive director of a Christian radio program, "Insight for Living," describes depression as "my own constant companion." She candidly shares personal struggles and victories.

"It is difficult to believe my life was darkened by depression for so long — fifteen years," Swindoll says. "Depression . . . black as a thousand midnights in a cypress swamp. Loneliness that is indescribable. Con fusion regarding God. Frustration with life and circumstances. The feeling that you have been abandoned, that you are worthless. Unlovable. The pain is excruciating."

By the same token, when a depressed person shares such depths of the soul, those closest to that person often are unsure how to handle it. Family and friends may feel rejected by what their depressed loved one says. In reality, the domination of negative feelings blurs a person's perspective. This confusion often leads that individual to shut out those closest to her.

During an onslaught of depression, one of our church members called me. She was crying and saying she wanted to divorce her husband. It was the first time I had spoken to this ordinarily reserved woman about her personal life. Through her tears she said, "I feel such unhappiness with Bert. I can't live with him any longer. He makes me feel terrible. What am I going to do?"

Later, her husband called to request prayer. He explained that their marriage was a good one. But his wife was experiencing fits of despair, a spirit of sadness and a constant, fierce swing of her emotions toward him. He mentally understood the fluctuation of her feelings when she was depressed, but it was hard to accept. It hurt when she turned on him. He longed for her to be more rational. He felt trapped by her depression cycles.

Admit Tendencies To Depression

Perhaps you're a Christian with recurring bouts of depression. Maybe you've been embarrassed by misconceptions in the Christian community about its causes. Let me offer you some reassurance. The depressed spirit isn't a result of sin or of self-pity alone, though they may be involved. In *Depression* by Don Baker, a psychiatric staff member said:

> Depression . . . has a cause. It's not the result of some mysterious visitation of the gods. It's an illness that's the result of certain biologic or social forces that in some complex way are acting detrimentally to your health. We must find those forces. They may be internal; they may be external. They may be physical; they may be mental. They may be real or they may be imagined, but we must find them, and when we do, we will recognize them and so will you. Then . . . you will get better.[1]

Uprooting these causes can reduce misconceptions in the minds of other people, remove humiliation from the hearts of the depressed, and help each of us deal with our own form of depression. We can regain our good spirits easier if we understand *why* we get depressed.

One thing we must understand: *Moods of sadness and loneliness are normal.* They are experienced by everyone.

Sin has stamped its mark on all of us. It has marred each earthly vessel. One of these marks of imperfection is the biological condition of experiencing chemical deficiencies in the brain which contribute to depression. In this case, accepting the fact of a chemical imbalance is the first step toward overcoming depression. However, there are also clear-cut cases of melancholic personalities and these tendencies must be dealt with as a weakness of temperament or a spirit prone to sadness.

In any case, admitting a problem with depression, rather than hiding it or denying it, is the starting point for conquering it.

Be Alert To Hormonal Effects

There are other physical causes for depression. Each of us women experience a form of depression at certain times due to biochemical changes and shifts. The medical writer, Hippocrates, in the fourth century B.C., described a strange sorrow in the mind of a new mother. We now refer to it as "post-partum blues."

I had a bout with the syndrome myself after Brenda, our first baby, was born. I remember bursting into tears the second day home. All Dave said was, "Good morning."

And I said, "I don't see anything good about it."

I cried from feelings of an inner sadness. The crying didn't last long, but my rationality seemed to have vanished. Medical professionals tell us that estrogens drop at the time of childbirth and progesterone is almost nonexistent — a dramatic decline from the high amount we produce during pregnancy. Tears and feelings of sadness are related to the body's rebalancing act after a baby is born. But while you are experiencing the blues, explanations only help to let you know you are normal — they don't do much to change your feelings.

The same is true about pre-menstrual tension, often referred to as P.M.S. There is a sharp progesterone drop four to five days before menstruation. This decline underlies mood changes which most of us are well aware of from monthly experience.

Menopause is a difficult transition for women. Margaret Mead referred to menopause as "the closing of the gates." The closing process involves the reduction of hormones. It happens over a long enough period of time so that the body gradually adjusts to the change — except for hot flashes and night sweats. During this phase some women experience depression, not due to the hormonal change but to the sense of loss — the loss of youth with its sexual appeal and reproductive capabilities.

Look For Obvious Signals

Loss, in any form, usually brings on depression. The most severe loss is probably felt through the tragedy of the death of someone we love.

A friend from Dallas called just before midnight one Thursday to relay the news of her husband's sudden death. The new widow recalled her last good-bye embrace and the love her husband had expressed in parting that morning. Before boarding the company airplane in the freshness of the October sunshine, he talked to her one last time on the phone. Warmly he said, "I'll be home for dinner." Instead came the news of the airplane crash and his death. With the warmth of his touch and the echo of his words still fresh in her mind, she called to request, "Could you and Dave come to Dallas? I would like Dave to do the funeral."

After I hung up, I tossed and turned in bed, reliving memories of my friend and her husband. I asked my Heavenly Father to comfort one of His beloved children. I was barely asleep when the telephone rang again. At the other end, I heard the tearful voice of my younger sister from Salt Lake City telling me her teen-aged daughter Sonia was killed just hours ago in an automobile crash. At first, I didn't say anything. I didn't pray; I only mumbled something. The shock sent a deep pain inside that was relieved only by crying.

It was difficult to listen to the details of the accident, and I could hear my brother-in-law sobbing in the background. The deep pain inwardly shook me as I thought of the warm, loving relationship he had had with his only daughter. She often would fix his breakfast in the morning and iron his shirt for work. I could see her smiling as she played tricks on him. I could hear her low giggle which always encouraged a hug from her father.

My sister continued to talk and cry and reminisce. Her greatest heartache seemed to be focused on the future. "There will be no college days, no beautiful wedding and no grandchildren born to my only daughter," she said between sobs. As I hung up the phone, I tried to grasp the reality: *Sonia is gone. Life, joy and happiness have temporarily vanished for my sister and her husband.*

I took my Bible with me on the flight to Salt Lake City. My daughter Debbie and I looked for comfort for our own hearts. Our source of peace came from the words of Jesus: "I am the resurrection and the life. He who believes in Me will live, even though he dies" (John 11:25).

This was our assurance that Sonia's faith in Christ would translate her securely to her Savior. While we on earth grieved, she was joyfully in heaven.

As Debbie and I examined the Scriptures, we came across another verse: "It is better to go to a house of mourning than to go to a house of feasting, for death is the destiny of every man; the living should take this to heart" (Ecclesiastes 7:2). We had gone to Sonia's house for a time of feasting and festivities a few years earlier. Our families had enjoyed snow skiing and snowmobiling together along with all the merriment of Christmas. As Debbie and I looked back at that time, we realized the truth of Ecclesiastes. The experience of mourning changed the direction of Debbie's life. She contemplated her own destiny and purpose.

We walked through those hours and days in Salt Lake City enveloped in sorrow. I empathized with the deep hurt of my sister, her husband, and their son. It pierced my heart. A question lingered in my mind: Would their hearts, or the heart of my dear widowed friend in Dallas, ever heal?

Allow Time For Emotional Healing

Grief is heaviness. It's the life-shaking sorrow over loss. It's like an inner weight. If you've experienced it, you know what I mean. The whole body reacts to the anguish, and it is relieved only by tears and then waves of sobbing. This is observed in the life of Abraham when he mourned the death of his wife, Sarah, and wept openly for her (Genesis 23:1).

Healing takes time. A period of bereavement is necessary. Psychologists say a year of grieving must pass for most widows, and sixteen months in the loss of a child, before survivors begin to adjust.

Grieving is an internal process which leads to emotional healing. Some cultures value wailing and tearing of hair and clothes as part of the process. Sorrow, like physical pain, has a purpose. Releasing tears and letting other people comfort us guides us through the first phase. This is necessary, but not always easy in our culture.

When another phase, anger, moves in, we must strike out in the right direction — not by lashing out at God, for He is our source of love and the one who heals the broken hearted; not by turning our anger inward, for this is self-destructive and leads to bitterness and continued hostile feelings; and not by harming other people with unruly anger, for this disrupts our relationships. Rather, our anger must be unleashed against sin. Hating the sin which causes disease and human wickedness is biblical. The Bible says, "Hate what is evil" (Romans 12:9). I learned to do this as I dealt with my niece's death.

My sister came to visit me two months after her daughter died. We walked the beach near my home. Against the roar of the wind, she shared her memories and feelings about Sonia and her death. Later, we were in the company of some skinny-legged sand pipers as the ocean had grown still. We stopped walking, and guietly talked about the hard things that plague every mind when death comes to one so young.

Did God will this accident to happen? Did He intend us to have this dark, heavy ache inside? As we reviewed portions of Scripture, we remembered that "every good and perfect gift is from above, coming down from the Father . . . who does not change like shifting shadows" (James 1:17). But we also recognized we live in a world stained by sin. Sickness, disease and death all exist because sin entered the world. Our sovereign God directs His created world to run on certain laws. Both a good person and an evil person live under these laws. Both suffer from the results of sin. Sometimes God miraculously intervenes — other times, in His infinite love and wisdom, He allows certain things to happen, and nobody knows why.

We talked about the Gospels. What Christ told His disciples holds true for us today: "You do not realize now what I am doing, but later you will understand" (John 13:7). He wants us to trust Him no matter what He allows. He wants us to realize that whatever He permits to happen is balanced with His compassion.

Learn From Jesus' Responses To Sorrow

Knowing Jesus understands and cares is the dynamic that helps us dispel depression. Jesus was "deeply moved in spirit and troubled" (John 11:33) when He saw Mary weeping. When He saw loved ones' hearts broken by the enemy of death, "Jesus wept" (John 11:35). Then He comforted Mary and Martha. His own heart aches with us when we hurt. He was "a man of sorrows and familiar with suffering" (Isaiah 53:3).

My sister and I talked about Sonia and her death until the sun began to set. We felt the refreshing cool December air of the tropics. Her downcast heart was uplifted by remembering how much Jesus cared about her personal sorrow. She was revitalized by remembering He would continue to be her comfort and her hope in the future.

Psychologists report that we don't give up those we love and are bonded to without great psychological and physiological anguish. Many sorrowing people turn to or increase the use of cigarettes, pills and alcohol to reduce their emotional hurt and despair.

The Bible offers an alternative to remaining in a deeply depressed state or to dulling the pain artificially. David fasted for seven days and spent the nights on the ground while his child was sick. Following his servant's announcement of the boy's death, "David got up from the ground. After he had washed, put on lotions and changed his clothes, he went into the house of the Lord and worshipped. Then he went to his own house, and at his request they served him food, and he ate" (2 Samuel 12:20). When the servants questioned his response, he said, "Can I bring him back again? I will go to him, but he will not return to me" (2 Samuel 12:23).

Expect Bouts Of Depression From Any Loss

Death isn't the only loss which can trigger depression.

A sense of loss can be experienced by a child, for example, when he is rejected by his mother. If your mother rejected or mistreated you, you have experienced the "loss" of your mother's love. A mother is the nurturer of a child's emotional needs. If she doesn't meet these needs, the child will have a problem with self-esteem. He can develop hostility toward and over-dependency on others. If there's been a loss of mother love, other losses will inflame the feeling of the original loss and deepen the accompanying depression.

Losing a job or status pulls up the anchor of security and leaves us adrift toward depression. Loss of a limb or use of a body function can be significantly painful. The breakup of a relationship by separation, divorce or the erection of emotional barriers is another kind of loss. This is one of the most common reasons for depression in women.

Most of us women have been trained to invest ourselves fully in relationships. This trait is virtually inborn. Therefore, broken or severed relationships can be as devastating to us as death. Maggie Scarf, a specialist on depression in women, says:

> It is around such "losses of love" that the depressive clouds tend to gather and to darken: important figures leaving or dying, a natural transition in life to relinquish an important love tie, a marriage that is ruptured, or simply growing progressively distant.[2]

I can well remember an experience of "love loss." We packed a van with our daughters' belongings, including clothes, bicycles, stereo set and treasured figurines, and drove the girls, eighteen and nineteen years old, to two different colleges. We unpacked half the van at one college for our younger daughter Debbie, the other half at Brenda's school. The seven-hour trip back home was a new experience for us. Usually the quietness was welcomed like a peaceful river. This time, however, the stillness of the empty van corresponded to the feelings in my inner being — and it wasn't pleasant.

Leaving the girls behind was like relinquishing two big chunks of myself. As I reflected on the past and the future, my heart hurt. I lay across the van seat wishing the rays of the sun would heal my heartache. Instead, it only made me think of sunny days gone by.

When we arrived home, the house was dark and still. As I glanced into the girls' bedrooms, the pain in my heart deepened. Everything was gone. Not just their personal items, but the life of their personalities had disappeared. As I showered before bed, my tears streamed with the flow of the water. I remembered their talking and giggling over the spray of this same shower a few short years ago.

Sleep wouldn't come. I felt as though life was over and I could never be happy again. With my eyes closed, I nostalgically reminisced — their birth details, their imaginative play times as preschoolers, their school work and birthday parties in preteen years, then their explosive junior high school years. It had seemed an overwhelming task to guide them through that era when it was clever to rebel against parents and all authority. Long hair, rock music, drugs and miniskirts pervaded our society and beckoned our daughters.

My thoughts raced ahead to more recent years. I saw that my life had revolved exclusively around their needs. I had been programmed to respond to those needs — from early morning when I drove them to their vocal group rehearsal until bedtime when the last problem was resolved.

After several hours, my tears had stopped and I had arrived at some conclusions. One phase of my motherhood was completed, mistakes included (and I had made plenty of them). I was thankful that I had been available to my girls during those days. The memory of the good times would always warm my heart. I said to myself, *Today begins a new passage for the girls, and for me. As they learn to fly alone, I must look for and dust off my dormant potential and try my own wings again.* Sleep finally came.

When the sun came up the next morning, I realized my daughters were just getting started, and I was starting over. That year I began counseling part-time, something I had prepared for but had never practiced professionally. I had two concerns about returning to work. First, I questioned whether or not I was competent to counsel after thirteen years out of school. Second, I wondered if I had the courage to change our family's rigid schedule. My husband and our thirteen-year-old son would have to make their own dinner plans on Thursday nights because therapy work was scheduled until nine o'clock. Initially, these were major concerns. Ultimately, my work required only a small adjustment for the three of us.

Returning to work proved to be therapeutic for me. It helped me stay afloat when I wanted to sink into the lonely, cut-off feelings of "losing" our daughters. In all honesty, my tendency would have been to demand more time from my busy husband or to get overly involved in the life of our son. But the emergence of my independent self was an effective weapon against that dependency. And it dealt with my depression as well, protecting our relationships.

What happens if we have to use all of our energy repairing and patching relationships? if we neglect our own potential while trying to keep others happy? We risk emotional hurt. If we don't achieve the confidence of self-sufficiency somewhere along the way, the chances are great we will eventually feel lonely, help-less, dependent — and then depressed. This can ruin the very relationships we are trying to keep.

The Bible describes a way to balance the dependency and the independency of our natures: "For each one should carry his own load" (Galatians 6:5); and "Carry each other's burdens, and in this way you will fulfill the law of Christ" (Galatians 6:2). This tension needs to be handled with action. Some of us need to summon the courage to push away from excessive dependency on our families. Others of us need to guard against the opposite pitfall of self-absorption.

Take Charge Of Conflicts

Ask yourself, Am I overly involved in my private world? Am I neglecting my primary tasks of caring for my family and home or of exercising my spiritual gifts? When a woman invests herself solely in a career or tends only to her personal desires, she will experience depression concerning the other areas which will be out of control. She will feel guilt about leaving respon-sibilities of the home dangling or shutting out time for ministry.

A twenty-three-year-old mother once told me how her depression was related to this tendency. Marlene was raised in an impoverished atmosphere. Her irres-ponsible mother tended to neglect her because of her work outside the home. Marlene said, "When I was a preschooler, my mother left me alone during the day without any available food. I vividly remember the hunger pains and the frustration of being unable to reach the refrigerator door handle. I would sit on the scummy, brown linoleum floor and cry. When I looked up, I saw stacks of dirty dishes which added to my already helpless feeling for I was too small to reach the sink and do them myself."

The sad feeling subsided when she was old enough to care for herself, but the depressed feelings returned when she had full responsibility for her own home. In a whimpering tone she explained, "When our family's dirty dishes pile high in the sink, I grow depressed. I go to my bedroom, pull the covers over my face and cry." Her early experiences and the feelings attached to them erupted powerfully in her mind and heart. It was difficult for this young woman to separate her present situation from her incapacitating childhood experiences. Here she was now, grown-up and able to do something about the dirty dishes. It was *her* responsibility now. What Marlene needed to learn was that she could overcome her depression by cultivating more disciplined actions. She could develop new behavior patterns associated with pleasant feelings.

Escaping under the covers is a symptom of depression, not a remedy for it. No amount of magic from the medicine cabinet can cure us either. Antidepressants treat chemical imbalance in the brain and can treat depression, but pills are misused if they are taken to eliminate unpleasant situations. If a woman has a marital disagreement, for example, and gets riled up inside over it, she may skirt the issue, take a pill and feel better — temporarily. But the relationship isn't any better. And the depression settles deeper.

There are healthier ways to deal with conflict than taking a pill and ignoring the situation. Marlene could examine her own responsibility in the conflict by asking, How is it my fault? How do I need to change?

It takes bravery to take responsibility. It's courageous to do first things first and care for the needs of the family — to throw back the covers and do the dishes, to walk away from the quick solutions with pills and to apologize for a selfish spirit.

Avoid Pitfalls Of Perfectionism

Depression is often linked with perfectionism. Do you strive for the unattainable? Are your goals — a perfect house, a perfect job situation, perfect kids and the perfect Christian life — set too high?

Perfectionism differs from the healthy pursuit of excellence, striving to do well at tasks within our reach. Depression moves in when the gap is too wide between our goals and standards, and what can be attained realistically. When the standard isn't met, the perfectionist blames herself and feels like a failure.

Each one of us enjoys walking barefoot across our freshly vacuumed carpet, or stepping into our freshly scrubbed kitchen, or dining at our own table elegantly set with fresh flowers from our garden. But there's no way we can live like this every day. It's an unrealistic standard unless we have household help or make it our top priority.

An aesthetic woman notices and appreciates beauty and fresh smells at home and works to please herself. Need she be compulsive about it? Certainly not. She can appreciate beauty without thinking her home must be spotless just to impress others.

Julie, one young mother in her mid-twenties, was a perfectionist but no one would have known. Her house was in shambles, and her children were unkempt. In high school she had been popular. She had a magnetic personality, unusually high morals and good grades, and was voted most likely to succeed.

During those years, Julie attained most of her goals and felt confident she was accepted by her peers. After a year of college, she happily married her old high school boyfriend who was already a college graduate. Within a year, she experienced mild depression — in an effort to impress her husband and mother-in-law, she was trying to maintain a perfect house and be the perfect wife.

She said, "My depression deepened after our babies were born, just one year apart. I became so depressed I didn't do anything. Lying in bed until noon, I listened to my babies cry in their wet, messy diapers, and I hoped my husband would come home for lunch and tend to them.

"I was aware that our household was in chaos. Dirty clothes were scattered everywhere. Unwashed cookware sat in the sink, yet I had no desire to do anything." Realizing her depressed state, she said, "I see the woman in Proverbs 31 as my standard. When I try to reach her level of doing everything and doing it perfectly, I fall so short that I feel like a failure as a keeper of our house and as a wife and mother, so I don't do anything or try anything. If I can't scrub the pans perfectly, I don't do them at all — or the wash, or the cleaning or anything."

Rather than seeing the woman in Proverbs as a model of principles for living, Julie envisioned a superwoman — someone she admired and wanted to emulate fully. She imagined becoming this ideal woman and dreamed of being filled with the energy, ambition and kindness of the woman's noble character. If only she excelled like this woman, she would feel as valuable and important as she had felt in high school. But the ideal seemed to keep rising like a star, always out of reach, and she felt herself falling further away, deeper into despair.

A perfectionist carries her high standards into her Christian life and easily experiences feelings of defeat. Witnessing, praying and loving are a way of life for the Christian woman, but a perfectionist, overly sensitive in spirit and plagued by a guilt of not doing enough, demands heavy duty on a long list of "have to's" from herself.

Lugging her "duty" baggage, she scans the heavens for God's approval. Like the earthly face of her mother or father who always remembered and pointed out her mistakes, the heavenly face is perceived as being turned away or as saying, "You can do better. You need to do more."

Consciously replacing the image of an earthly, dissatisfied face with an accurate picture of Christ is the first step the perfectionistic Christian needs to attempt. Try it. Picture an open, honest, sharing relationship with Christ, the one who loves you more than any earthly person can. See yourself walking alone with Him in a peaceful, comfortable setting, maybe along a country lane under sunny skies. Tell Him about yourself, your troubles and your desires. Confess to Him the personal pride of wanting to do better than everybody else and the resentments you have carried.

Focus for a moment on this confession. Know your sin is forgiven, and accept that forgiveness. Picture your sin disappearing before your eyes, like pebbles down a mountain cliff...gone. We see in 1 John 1:7, "But if we walk in the light...the blood of Jesus purifies us from every sin." Finally, listen to the words of Jesus' offer about how we can work together in friendship with Him: "Come to me all ye that are weary and burdened and I will give you rest. Take my yoke upon you and learn from Me, for I am gentle and humble in heart and you will find rest for your souls. For My yoke is easy and My burden is light" (Matthew 11:28-30).

Deal With Guilt Feelings

Guilt feelings are one of the leading factors in depression. You may or may not be guilty of a sin. How can you tell? If your guilt feelings are connected to disobeying God's laws in a specific act or attitude, you'll know your guilt is valid. If your feelings aren't linked to violating any specific biblical standard but stem from an attitude of self-condemnation, you're experiencing false guilt. We can begin to resolve our conflicts with guilt feelings when we are able to differentiate between real and false guilt.

When we forsake our sin and ask God's forgiveness, He forgives us and we begin to heal. The psalmist David is a classic example of a person who experienced healing from valid guilt. Listen to how he describes his guilty feelings after his adulterous affair: "When I kept silent, my bones wasted away through my groaning all day long. For day and night your hand was heavy upon me; my strength was sapped as in the heat of summer. Then I acknowledged my sin to you and did not cover up my iniquity. I said, 'I will confess my transgressions to the Lord' — and you forgave the guilt of my sin" (Psalm 32:3-5).

Sin separates us from God and from other people. It agitates our nerves and robs our hearts of peace. In His unfailing love God waits for us to come to Him. So why don't we? Out of pride or wrong thinking, we're tempted to resolve the guilt feelings in our own way. We try to hide the sin, rationalize and deny the fact of sin, blame others and the circumstances, or punish ourselves.

Lucille, a middle-aged woman, was experiencing little intimacy and excitement in her relationship with her husband. In a close working situation with a seemingly successful, divorced man, she felt the arousal of warm feelings and an attraction for him. She maneuvered a secret affair which she found exciting and praised as "next to heaven." But the excitement of passion was interspersed with feelings of guilt. She knew she had broken her trust with her husband and had disobeyed one of God's commands.

In time, Lucille's lover found another woman. All that remained were the ashes of a dead romance and the agony of guilt. She experienced the humiliation of rejection. In shame she hid her face from God, distancing herself from her source of strength. In utter despair, she wanted to die; a bottle of pills seemed the answer. Some Christian friends discovered her slumped over the steering wheel of her car and by their quick action were able to save her life.

This was the turning point. With time, healing came. Lucille's recovery was slow and painful. Many months later she faced the Lord, asking His forgiveness. She eventually sought her husband's forgiveness as well.

God desires truth in our inner being. When we face the truth of our wrong-doing, depression lifts and the joy of salvation returns (Psalm 51:6, 12). God, in love, waits to set us free. He *promises* forgiveness in response to confession (1 John 1:9).

Whether our hearts are hardened by the sin of an extramarital affair or by bitterness about apparent unfairness in our relationships and circumstances, God is compassionate. He forgives us when we turn to Him. The hardness melts. He transforms our downcast spirit and gloomy countenance to a brightness like rays of sunshine after the rain.

Handle With Creativity

Two women, close to the same age, chose a creative way to push back despair. Both were Christians — one since she was a child, the other for only a few years — both mothers with teenagers, both doctors' wives, both with the same enemy, cancer. The two of them decided to walk together through their dreadful illness. As a result, their lives became bonded in an unusual friendship.

Who could understand better a person's feelings of losing health, or the extreme sickness accompanying chemotherapy treatments, or the heaviness of heart when looking into the future, than a friend who was experiencing the same dreaded disease?

The women spent each Monday together at one of their homes. Beyond merely talking about their feelings, they ministered to each other with meaningful Scripture, praying and praising God. After their worship, each encouraged the other to be brave in tackling a difficult project they had decided upon. In the same room, but alone in their own chairs, they wrote letters to each of their children. Each letter contained the mother's memories of the child, lessons from her own life and words of love for that child. The letters were placed in a treasure chest, to be opened when the child reached a certain age if the mother were no longer living. One of the mothers with a young daughter penned words of her own feelings when she had turned thirteen, and explained how Colossians 3:23 had helped her.

Walking together helped these two women cast out their deepest darkness. They focused outside themselves — on each other, on their children and on God. They prepared for the future as they built a treasure chest in heaven and on earth. One friend's eyes now mist with grief over the loss of the other; her companion is now in heaven. The best part of their journey together was growing more Christ-like, but one is still growing and the other is now complete, like Him.

Check Your All-Around Fitness

We've traced common causes of depression and dealt with key suggestions to help the troubled spirit. *I can get better* is what we need to tell ourselves when we're feeling down. Spending time with God lifts us out of the deepest slump. We talk to Him in prayer, He talks to us through His Word.

For those who experience prolonged depression or recurring episodes, preventative steps need to be taken.

Ongoing therapy for the continued well-being of the depressed personality can prevent more severe problems. A support person or group which understands the destructive potential can aid in the fight to stay on an even keel.

But our greatest ally is our secure relationship with Christ. When loneliness seems to swallow us up, or our thoughts are confused and we feel unable to cooperate with God, Jesus understands. That is comforting. He keeps loving us and reaching out to us. He is longing and waiting for us to spend time with Him again.

Each of us can benefit by periodically reviewing the following helps. These tips are especially helpful if you have a melancholic temperament — sensitive, reflective, moody, perfectionistic. Check yourself *before* depression moves in. Use these suggestions to offset its control.

A BALANCED-LIFE CHECKLIST: Secrets To Staying Fit and Offsetting Depression

Physical

[   ] 1. Have a regular check-up by a physician.
[   ] 2. Eat a proper diet.
[   ] 3. Follow a regular pattern of sleep.
[   ] 4. Exercise regularly, at least three times a week.
[   ] 5. Allow for hormonal changes during your menstrual cycle, after the birth of a baby and during menopause.
[   ] 6. Be aware of the availability of anti-depressants for severe depression.

Mental/Emotional

[   ] 1. See yourself clearly and accept yourself as valuable because God says you are.

[   ] 2. Know your strengths; accept your imperfections and face your problems.

[   ] 3. Strive to do well and reach for realistic goals, not to attain superiority but to achieve personal confidence.

[   ] 4. Focus on your personal behavior, not just on feelings. Feelings are neither right nor wrong; what we do with our feelings is what makes them right or wrong.

[   ] 5. Learn to take care of yourself; don't lean on others.

[   ] 6. Spend time with your family and friends and do something nice for others.

[   ] 7. Speak up; don't withdraw; express your personal ideas, feelings and desires. Learn to use the word *no.*

[   ] 8. Structure each day to include work, relaxation and worship.

[   ] 9. Whistle while you work.

Spiritual

[   ] 1. Encounter God in a personal relationship through His Son, Jesus Christ (John 1:12).

[   ] 2. Seek forgiveness for any sin which separates you and God or you and others. Follow David's example (Psalm 32).

[   ] 3. Trust God for His love and healing in your loss (Psalm 147:3).

[   ] 4. Strengthen your relationship with Him in quiet times where He can give you perspective like He gave to David when he went into the sanctuary (Psalm 73:17).

[   ] 5. Expel anger and bitterness by writing it out or telling it to a trusted person — to the Lord, if possible, in the manner of Hannah (1 Samuel 1:10).

[ ] 6. Refuse negative thinking which perpetuates depression. A negative response to a person or situation can trigger a downward spiral. This is what happened to Jonah who griped and brooded until he wanted to die (Jonah 4:3-9).

[ ] 7. Memorize God's Word. Replace negative thinking with its promises, including the following verses:

> Psalm 23:4, "Even though I walk through the valley of the shadow of death, I will fear no evil, for Thou art with me."
> Romans 15:13, "May the God of hope fill you with all joy and peace as you trust in Him."
> Isaiah 44:22, "I have swept away your offenses like a cloud, your sins like the morning mist."
> Hebrews 13:15, "Let us continually offer to God a sacrifice of praise — the fruit of lips that confess His name."
> 2 Corinthians 4:8,9, "We are hardpressed on every side but not crushed, perplexed but not in despair, persecuted but not abandoned, struck down but not destroyed."

[ ] 8. Study God's method of working with Elijah in overcoming depression (1 Kings 19:1-15).

[ ] 9. Pray and ask for God's help when the demand seems too heavy, just like Moses when he cried out to God about his heavy load (Numbers 11:14).

[ ]10. Praise God for His blessings. This is the best therapy for a heavy spirit. Praise Him, adore Him for who He is just as Mary did: "My soul praises the Lord and my spirit rejoices in God, my Saviour" (Luke 1:46-47).

[　]11. Continue praising God by using a hymnal and singing a song such as "No One Ever Cared For Me Like Jesus."

[　]12. Search for a friend to share your heart with. Then you can dispel the loneliness and fight the relentless attacker, depression — together.

6

Why Do I Get Upset So Easily?

*Thinking the right thoughts
is the dynamic for mastering anger*

We were on vacation, and one evening after dinner Dave carelessly said to me, "I think you are too weak to hit a tennis ball." Irritation twinged, then churned inside me.

He had challenged me in a sensitive area. I had not given much thought to my own physical fitness since school days, but now I was suddenly forced to think about it. I mentally defended myself, thinking of all the ways I displayed my strength. *Doesn't Dave know how much energy it takes to care for our three children and our home? How can he say I'm weak?*

Inwardly I felt put down by my husband. The more I thought about it, the more irritated I became. I felt as I had when a church committee member once ridiculed a misspelled word in my letter to parents. I remembered another painful occasion when an expert seamstress discovered a pucker in the sleeve of my selfmade dress. She put her finger on it and talked about the mistake in front of a group of friends. I didn't say anything to the women in either situation, but I recalled feeling irritated enough to want to say, "Well, you're certainly not perfect either."

Now I wanted to shoot back at my husband, "Don't think you're so great just because you play sports and are strong." But I withheld those words and went to bed. As I lay there, I could see myself hitting a tennis ball with explosive strength.

Irritations Arouse Anger

Remember the last time you were irritated? How did you respond? When someone told you how to do something their way — like how to drive a car — did they imply your way was inferior? How did you feel? What did you do? Irritations arouse anger. How we respond to the irritations either fuel or dispel the anger.

Would learning to play golf frustrate you? or trying to relate to your husband? or rearing your children? Whenever there are obstacles to reaching our goals or obstacles blocking our selfish desires, we can expect frustration. Anger probably will follow.

Frustrations Provoke Anger

Everyday occurrences hold the potential of frustrating us and provoking anger. It doesn't take much — the breakdown of our dishwasher, poor communication with our children, or a telephone call interrupting our dinner.

Perhaps you've experienced crawling into your bed after an especially busy day — pulling the fresh-smelling sheet and the soft quilt up to your chin, adjusting your weary body just right and drifting into a wonderful sleep, mumbling, "Thank goodness — tomorrow I have important things to do, and I need to get up early, and I want to feel good all day." But your deep, luscious sleep was interrupted by a blinding light, the slam of a door, and the feel of the mattress rolling away from you. Your husband was coming to bed and you were jolted wide awake. After that, you lay in bed trying to go back to sleep, but it was useless — sleep had left you.

You probably became frustrated. You may have seethed with angry feelings.

Hurt Feelings Stir Up Anger

Irritations and frustrations can stir up anger — and so can hurt feelings. When a friend apparently snubs you, or friends make unkind comments behind your back, you feel hurt. When cutting remarks come back to us from someone we care about, those words, like insect bites, sting.

What do you do? Do you say anything?

Some hurtful experiences are severe enough to linger and become embedded in the memory.

Heather remembers the day her father blurted out, "Your older sister is getting prettier than you are." She was just ten years old. The insult was like a dart that stabbed her, and the wound was followed by a flood of anger. She didn't say anything to her father or sister, but the anger became intense and she wanted to lash out at both of them. Instead she held it all inside and felt the anger swelling up, seeming to push against her skin, searching for an outlet.

Harboring hurt feelings leads easily to anger. It can become intense enough to implant evil thoughts. I know of one resentful wife who said, "My husband has been cheating on me for a year and — can you believe it? — it's with my best friend. At first I was hurt but now I *hate* him! I feel like buying a revolver and killing him!"

Was it wrong for this woman to feel angry because her husband cheated on her? How do you feel about yourself and your anger?

Anger Is . . .

You may have the same notion I acquired by growing up in an environment where it was wrong to get "mad." Our family and friends called anger the "nasty emotion." Anger was taboo. Though we considered it wrong to get mad, I heard my Aunt Polly say that it was OK to be "vexed." I realize now that Aunt Polly simply changed the word to justify the feeling.

We may label some feelings "mad," "vexed," "hostile," "resentful" or "bitter." Whatever we call it, we are referring to the same emotion — anger. We all experience angry feelings.

Anger Energizes

Anger is an emotional/physical response to an experience or situation. We may feel anger at various levels — from a low level of irritation to a high level of fury or rage.

When we become angry, our body goes to work. With an automatic, physiological reaction, it transforms emotion to a surge of energy. When anger is full-blown, it infuses the entire body, preparing it for action. If we released that energy — unrestrained by what is right or wrong — we would be capable of hurting others with put-downs and curses, or we could be violent and actually injure someone physically.

However, the energy generated by anger can be harnessed and rechanneled. It can be used for good if it nudges us to talk out conflicts with our husbands. It can benefit our parenting role if it prompts us to teach our children values from a strong conviction.

Anger *can* be useful. Fighting evil by either crusading against injustices or preaching against sin is a positive way to borrow energy from anger.

Consider other ways anger energy can be recycled.

A woman's blood can boil, thrusting her into positive action, forcing her to take part in righting some wrongs: when a person who has been invested with trust purposely mishandles money belonging to the elderly; when adults abuse children; when the innocent are taken advantage of; or when the suffering are ignored.

In the Gospels we read how Jesus used the energy of anger in response to the evil He saw. "Jesus entered the temple area and began driving out those who were buying and selling there. He overturned the tables of the money changers and the benches of those selling doves, and would not allow anyone to carry merchandise through the temple courts" (Mark 11:15,16).

Anger Can Be Explosive

Anger is like a match. Matches are readily available — mine are kept inside my kitchen drawer. When I strike a match, a flame bursts forth. I can use that flame to light a candle for beauty or a fire for warmth. But I can also use it to light a stick of dynamite, unleashing its power to ruin and to demolish.

Anger's flame is most often used destructively. It bursts out and energizes us with the power to destroy people as surely as dynamite blows up buildings.

Destructive Anger Tactics

What happens when you return home from a party where your husband talked to every woman but you and gave them his full attention and his finest smile? If you take his action as an insult or threat, you also felt some anger stirring. Then what happens?

If you choose to clam up and stuff your angry feelings deep inside, you may discredit yourself. As you push down your feelings you will feel hurt. You'll blame yourself by entertaining thoughts like, *I didn't look good enough or behave good enough to deserve my husband's attention.*

A woman who stuffs her feelings tends to become withdrawn and depressed.

The feelings don't die inside the one who stuffs them. Neither do they remain hidden. Rather, they seep out sideways. She turns a cold shoulder to her partner, uninterested in his sexual advances. Or her anger may be diverted to other sideways attacks. It's usually subtle, such as stubbornly refusing to do what her partner asks or making sarcastic remarks. In this case, instead of confronting him about his flirtatious behavior, she may blame him for leaving his shoes under the kitchen table. Or she may attack the children or pick on other people.

Some women handle their anger like my grandmother did her money. My mother remembers that, when she was a girl, my grandmother placed coins in a sugar bowl and saved them until there were enough to buy a surprise for a family member.

Anger-savers carefully collect grievances and hurtful experiences. They put them in their memory bank until they have enough to pour out in a pay-back-get-even plan. Then they recount each one in the presence of their surprised partner. They want to hurt their partner or make that person feel inferior since they have been hurt and made to feel inferior themselves.

Jean Harris, Headmistress of Madeira School, one of the most prestigious preparatory schools in the country, was an anger-saver. Her hurts were recounted on ten pages of Madeira School stationery, and addressed to her lover, Dr. Herman Tarnower, a Scarsdale diet cardiologist. She related the aching hurt when he didn't call her. She reiterated the humiliating feelings when the small, balding man abused her as she played mistress. Her memory bank was overflowing with angry feelings from being used and discarded. This attractive, socially sophisticated woman surprised the doctor — she killed him. She shot him to death.

Some angry feelings may just be stored away in a hidden place, deep inside us. In one section of the basement in our home in the Midwest, a friend built a pegboard partition, making an extra room for us. He made a small sign and hooked it on the pegboard. It said "Junk Room" and the room lived up to its name. Anything we didn't know what to do with would be tossed inside the junk room, hidden from ourselves and others, and forgotten. It bothered me when it got so full I couldn't open the door, so I had to sort through everything. I gathered up bundles of junk and threw them out. I felt good about getting rid of those bundles. It made room for worthwhile storage.

Stored up angry feelings or grudges are collected in the junk rooms of our inner being. This pile of covered up junk irritates us and causes depression. It robs us of a place for pleasant memories. Stored up anger is one cause of depression. This emotion unconsciously turns inward as we attempt to deny it to ourselves and others.

Ask any depressed woman, Why are you angry? and she will probably answer, I am not angry. This is a signal. She needs help to wade through the junk room in order to find the anger. Then she can begin to eliminate it.

Act, Don't React

The woman who blows up can launch a vicious verbal attack — either sarcastically or in a straightforward manner. She is out of control. Her anger can explode like dynamite...powerfully...destructively. The woman who blows up usually begins by throwing out negative comments, then may turn to blaming and calling the offender names. If she allows the anger to escalate, she may shout and use abusive language, and she may even resort to physical violence. After she blows up, the woman may feel sorry and apologetic, but some irreparable damage will remain. Unfortunately, uncontrolled words and actions are irreversible. They leave ourselves and others wounded.

The Bible describes a man named Cain who became angry. God accepted Cain's younger brother's offering and did not look with favor on Cain's offering.

> Then the LORD said to Cain, "Why are you angry? Why is your face downcast? If you do what is right, will you not be accepted? But if you do not do what is right, sin is crouching at your door; it desires to have you, but you must master it." Now Cain said to his brother Abel, "Let's go out to the field." And while they were in the field, Cain attacked his brother Abel, and killed him (Genesis 4:6-8).

God offered Cain an opportunity to respond and talk with Him about his anger. God asked, "Why are you angry?" But Cain chose to ignore God. This disobedient act opened the door to sin. He paid no attention to God's warning, and, as a result, anger got the upper hand and mastered *him*.

When someone asks, Why are you angry? do you say, "I'm not angry" or, "Leave me alone"? Or do you open up and talk about it? Listen to the warning: *You must master sin.*

Right-Thinking Strategies

When a person causes anger to flare up in your heart, as it did in Cain's, you can give in and allow it to blaze wildly, fueling it with negative thinking, or you can choose to reflect calmly on how to smother the flame and bring the anger under control. *Pause and think before you act* is the guideline. When anger-arousing situations arise:

Think. Before doing anything, stop and think of what the Bible says. "Be slow to anger" (James 1:19).

Pray. Ask God to help you with positive rather than negative thinking. Instead of focusing on the other person and his behavior, center your thoughts on God and your belongingness to Him and His faithfulness to you. After the anger energy has cooled down, ask God for wisdom as to what to discuss with the other person.

Think of the best way to express how you feel. If the offender is your spouse, be prepared before you go to sleep to communicate what you think or feel (Ephesians 4:26). He will then know how you perceive his behavior and how you are affected by what he says and does.

Consider your tone of voice. "A gentle answer turns away wrath, but a harsh word stirs up anger" (Proverbs 15:1). A soft voice is easier to listen to and is more apt to encourage a spirit of love in the heart of the listener.

Speak the truth rather than putting up a smokescreen by saying something to protect your hurting ego (Ephesians 4:25). Avoid words of put-down and self-defense. Tell the truth as to how you feel and what you need. Do you know what you need from your husband in an insecure moment at a social event? Think about it and try to put it into words. "I need you to _____ (put your arm around me some time during the

party)." When we communicate directly what we
feel and what we need, we feel emotionally close
to our partner and we also feel respect for ourselves.

Mastering anger includes not only right thinking to
offset blow-ups, but also avoiding the entrapment of
clamming up. Withdrawing into silence can lead to a
host of other problems, for instance, headaches in the
bedroom, negative comments in public, and in time,
irrelevant quarrels.

I have some bittersweet memories of our newlywed
days. Sometimes when Dave would come home late
after playing a game or discussing church business, I
would feel hurt. It seemed to me that I was unimportant
to him because he neglected to call. Instead of talking
about it, I responded by withdrawing into silence. I
thought a nice wife shouldn't be angry and assumed
I would feel better the next day. When we went to
bed, I built an invisible wall that separated us from
any physical contact. Though we were only inches
apart and I could feel the warmth of his body, we
were miles apart emotionally. The heavy silence burned
my ears. The next morning nothing would be changed.
If anything, the hurt would be deeper and I would
feel more miserable.

With time, I finally learned it was not a sin to be
angry, but that it's possible to sin in my anger. Paul
commands, "In your anger do not sin" (Ephesians
4:26). I was wrong to clam up. When I refused to
express my feelings, I wasted energy. Love and joy
were blocked. Now, when I begin to feel angry, by an
act of the will I try to release the resentment. With a
few words I can set into motion communication which
is direct and truthful. I have learned to control my
anger. I can build up our relationship when I admit,
"I feel _____ (neglected)." Or I say,

"I need for you to (call me when you are late)." This is the method the New Testament teaches us to use in order to master anger. "Do not let the sun go down while you are still angry and do not give the devil a foothold" (Ephesians 4:26,27).

Yielding to this principle is the mark of a mature Christian woman. She dispels her feelings of anger in a controlled, truthful manner. No camouflaging. No pressure-cooker tactics. No explosive blow-ups.

Anger Can Become Sin

Saving up anger, with the intention of getting even with someone, is as destructive as blowing up and clamming up.

The Bible says, "Do not repay anyone evil for evil. Do not take revenge, my friends, but leave room for God's wrath, for it is written: 'It is mine to avenge; I will repay, says the Lord' " (Romans 12:17-19).

An evil woman in the New Testament disregarded God's standard. "So Herodius nursed a grudge against John and wanted to kill him" (Mark 6:19). By clever maneuvering she had John the Baptist executed. She justified her actions because John the Baptist had told her husband, Herod, that it was not lawful for him to marry her for she was the wife of his brother. She was irritated with the words of John the Baptist and the high regard Herod held for him — so she used her own means to pay him back.

I can still recall what I *really* felt when, as a seven-year-old, I said, "I'm sorry" to Fay. I said the proper words, but I didn't dare look at her face because I was so mad at her. Fay was nineteen and she helped my mother during the summer months at our Diamond Lake cottage. She told mother a story about me that was not true and mother told me to apologize. I did, but my heart was crying out, "Unfair!" And I certainly didn't forgive her — I felt I had a *right* to be mad at her.

Choose Relief — Avoid Resentment

When have you experienced unfair treatment? Was it due to the color of your skin? Or did your parents abuse you? Perhaps you cry out with the psalmist, "All day long I have been plagued; I have been punished every morning" (Psalm 73:14). You may be tempted to lash out in anger toward others — and even at God — for life's injustices. Maybe you have suffered mistreatment as your husband cruelly misused his God-given authority and superior strength.

One woman jointly owned a business and worked every day in partnership with her husband for over twenty years. She managed the secretarial and bookkeeping end. Without any discussion, he deceitfully got her signature and one day he sold the business. The next morning, as he ate the breakfast she served him, he announced the sale. In a dictatorial manner, he heartlessly stated that the new company had replaced her with a younger secretary. That morning she tearfully related the story to me over the telephone. What could she do?

In the Bible, a woman named Hannah was faced with a situation of similar difficulty. She lived in a polygamous home where there was jealousy and domestic quarreling. Hannah's husband, Elkanah, loved her and publicly honored her, but the Lord had closed her womb. Since they had no children, Elkanah married a second wife named Peninnah who bore him children. Peninnah was jealous of Elkanah's superior affection for Hannah. Scripture says that Peninnah "kept provoking her [Hannah] in order to irritate her. This went on year after year. Whenever Hannah went up to the house of the LORD her rival provoked her until she wept and would not eat" (1 Samuel 1:6,7).

Evidently Peninnah annoyed and tantalized Hannah unmercifully, poking fun at her and stirring her up inwardly. What could Hannah do in this hemmed-in situation? Were there any alternatives? Would she save up her resentment and plot a murder like Herodius did?

Hannah did not resort to getting even with her adversary. Rather, she found relief from her torment in a way that God has provided for us when we experience unjust treatment. "In bitterness of soul, Hannah wept much and prayed to the Lord" (1 Samuel 1:10).

She cried out to God, and she let go of her bitterness. This out-pouring of the resentment in her soul prepared the way for her request to God for a son. Following this removal of bitterness, God opened her womb and she conceived and gave birth to Samuel.

When Hannah gave God control of her situation, He worked things out for her good. Knowing God was in control gave her security, and the same dynamic of knowing He is in control secures us and enables us to master anger. Romans says that all things work together for good to those of us who love God (see Romans 8:28).

Hanging on to resentment, no matter what the situation or mistreatment by others, will hurt us. It will result only in misery. Nursing self-pity, exploding in rage, or plotting ways to get even, will become a pattern of life. Most of all, these attitudes and actions will block an otherwise open pathway to God.

Suzanne wrote me a letter saying, "I'm to the point where I hardly ever pray and I very seldom read my Bible. My close fellowship with the Lord is nil, and I know why. It's because of another person that just grinds me. When I see her or hear her I just can't stand it." If we carry around resentment and an unforgiving spirit, we are weighed down, tied to misery.

Forgiving does not mean that we have to take the blame or even to say that the person who hurt us was right. Instead it's like canceling a debt that someone owes us. Forgiveness is canceling, through an act of the will, all the evil things your mother-in-law did when you were first married, or crossing out the wrong your sister did you when she manipulated until she acquired the bulk of your parents' estate.

Come to God like Hannah did. Ask Him to forgive your resentment. Pray for the person you are bitter toward. State what you need to forgive this person for. (For example, *I forgive my mother-in-law for her possessiveness and my sister for her manipulation*.)

If you habitually look for, then talk about, people's faults, desiring to make yourself look better, you are tearing others down and hurting them and fanning the flame of anger. It is essential to part with a hostile spirit as well as with resentment. Figuratively cough it up and out in the presence of God. What a relief to get rid of an angry spirit. Parting with hostility will allow you to let God's love pour into your heart and flow through you to others.

We have been considering right thinking as the dynamic for mastering anger. Now here is a checklist of questions to help you discover where right thinking will help you most in dealing with your own anger.

RIGHT-THINKING CHECKLIST

ASK YOURSELF NOW

> Am I angry?
> Am I hanging on to anger because:
> [ ] I hurt and want to get even?
> [ ] I enjoy the strength and power from anger's energy?

[ ] I use it as a shield of defense against depression and feelings of worthlessness?

BEFORE YOU GO TO SLEEP TONIGHT

[ ] 1. Thank God for His forgiveness toward you.
[ ] 2. Seek His forgiveness
   • for your blow-ups of uncontrolled anger;
   • for saving up anger with the intention of striking back;
   • for denying the existence of anger;
   • for hiding anger in the junk room of the deepest part of your inner being.
[ ] 3. Ask God to show you how your actions frustrate or irritate your husband, your children, or others. Ask yourself, Am I
   • too demanding?
   • too quick to give advice?
   • too quick to criticize?
   • too possessive?
[ ] 4. Ask God to replace critical attitudes with characteristics of His Spirit, including the fruit of love, patience, kindness, and self-control (see Galatians 5:22,23).
[ ] 5. Do you need to ask any family member to forgive you? If it is possible, do it now.

WHAT TO DO WITH YOUR ANGER TOMORROW

[   ] 1. To *build* intimacy in marriage,
- communicate with your husband;
- honestly express how you feel;
- use a controlled manner at the right time and place to point out what he does that irritates, insults or frustrates you;
- keep your self-respect and respect for your husband intact;
- teach your children right from wrong;
- correct them in a controlled manner;
- teach them principles from God's Word, including how to handle their own anger.

[   ] 2. Memorize verses on controlling your anger. Here are some starters:

Everyone should be quick to listen, slow to speak and slow to become angry (James 1:19).

In your anger do not sin: Do not let the sun go down while you are still angry, and do not give the devil a foothold (Ephesians 4:26, 27).

Do not take revenge, my friends, but leave room for God's wrath, for it is written:

"It is mine to avenge; I will repay," says the Lord (Romans 12:19).

[   ] 3. Control your temper. "Get rid of all bitterness, rage, and anger, brawling and slander, along with every form of malice. Be kind and compassionate to one another, forgiving each other, just as in Christ God forgave you" (Ephesians 4:31,32).

Where do you especially need to do this —
- with your in-laws?
- with people at work?
- in a neighborhood or church situation?
- with family members?

[   ] 4. Make love your aim.
"Love is patient, love is kind. It does not envy.... It is not rude...it is not easily angered, it keeps no record of wrongs" (1 Corinthians 13:4,5).
- Reaffirm your love for the one who "done you wrong" (2 Corinthians 2:7,8).
- Be willing to forgive seventy times seven those you have disagreed with or been jealous of (Matthew 18:22).

7

Why Do I Give In To . . .?

*Exalting God
is the dynamic for overcoming the enemy*

Dear Sue,

I was planning on going to sleep. I had put my Bible study lesson down and had my prayer time, but as I lay my head down, a light went on in my mind. It had to do with the lesson based on our battle with Satan. I got a picture of my battles — the attacks come in the form of a Big Mac, a pizza, a hot fudge sundae, and Oreos.

Earlier in the evening I was watching television and I saw the commercial for Oreo Cookies and Cream ice cream. I love Oreos, especially frozen ones. I called some grocery stores to see if they had any because I had such a strong urge to get some. When I couldn't find any, I didn't know if television should be banned, or just all food commercials.

Food is my battleground — how can God use me if I can't control what goes in my mouth? A touch of depression makes it worse, for I have a bad habit of reaching for food when I'm feeling down. I'm concerned also about my nutritional intake. Even though it's summer and good fruits are available, I don't easily reach for them. Instead I reach for chocolates, which I love, and chocolate makes depression worse for it chemically potentiates depression. Why don't I just turn away from my poor eating habits?

I'm a binger — not a binger-purger, just a binger — who gets fatter and fatter and more thoroughly disgusting.

Watching me binge would be funny if it weren't so sad. Spending too much money. Eating too much. I wonder if my habit is linked chemically to something in my brain. Will science one day help me be free from those almost uncontrollable urges? It's strange. I could get over marijuana (which I truly loved and occasionally still think about), and cigarettes, and my garbage mouth (which still needs some improving). But food, well, that's different. You can't just go cold turkey and quit eating. It is the ultimate discipline for me. Why do I have such a hard time permanently changing my food habits? Is there help for my overeating by understanding the full armor of God? What about a memory verse? If I thought it would help, I would do a counted cross-stitch sampler and send it to myself. Do you have any ideas?

                                                    A friend.

Overeating is a problem many women can identify with. Uncontrollable urges for food characterize the secret habits of those who overeat. This results in feeling guilty and socially ill at ease. Overeating is perhaps more threatening to a Christian woman. Her appearance reflects the message, "You are defeated in your goal to honor God."

In the first six chapters we have seen that a Christian woman is secure because she belongs to God. He fills her inner life with purpose as she grows in the image of Christ. Her longings for peace, joy and love — opposed to anxiety, depression and anger — are met as she follows the steps of cooperation with God.

Strong Temptations

We wish all would go smoothly and we could live gloriously like Eve before the fall, but we are faced with a problem. There is an inner pull in our natural appetite that makes us want to do all sorts of things. This pull urges us to go beyond common-sense boundaries. The desire for food, for example, is born out of a need to nourish our body — but cravings for food in excess of our need delude us into thinking that more would bring emotional satisfaction.

Normal desires for pleasure can be heightened to insatiable levels, enticing us to set aside moral standards.

The Bible calls these strong urges temptations. They are common. Christians should expect them. Even Jesus experienced temptation. The danger is that temptation's persuasive power can lead to sin. James 1:14,15 says, "But each one is tempted when, by his own evil desire, he is dragged away and enticed. Then, after desire has conceived, it gives birth to sin."

Temptations are at work in us in three main areas: the desires of the flesh, the desires of the eyes, and the pride of life. John descirbes these three natural desires as "the cravings of sinful man, the lust of his eyes and the boasting of what he has and does" (1 John 2:16).

Lust

The peasant woman of the village of Sychar yielded to pleasures in excess. Jesus, a Jewish stranger to her, sat by Jacob's well and told her of her life of indulging in her desires — He knew of her five husbands and present live-in partner. Giving in to her cravings gave her a reputation as the town harlot. The attractive woman knew the shameful effects. When she needed water, she walked the hot streets alone in mid-day to the well in order to escape the gossiping women who enjoyed drawing their water in the cool of the day.

This Samaritan woman said yes to a pull toward excess in fulfilling her pleasure. She succumbed to fleshly temptation. Though few of us can identify with her numerous marriages and affairs, there may be one person you are attracted to who is not your marriage partner. Do you yearn to see an old boyfriend, or your friend's husband, or the man you work with? Is there an inner coaxing to be with this man — just to talk — and then see what happens?

One Sunday, a friend of mine who had been happily married for five years and had two children stopped me after church to relate an experience she had had that week. A boy she had seriously dated in high school called and asked her if she would meet him. Six years earlier he had shocked her when he suddenly joined the service. She began dating others and eventually fell in love with and married her husband.

She started crying as she said "When my old boyfriend called last week my heart started to pound. As soon as I heard his voice, the old passionate feelings came rushing back. I wanted to see him more than I could ever say. I told him I would have to think about it. What should I do?"

What would you do? Would seeing him satisfy her? Chances are that the encounter would create a desire for more of him. Then an inner coaxing would persist until she either broke her commitment to her husband or developed a barrier between herself and him.

We are not all tempted in the same area. But we are all sinful and each of us has experienced the pull to go back into sin after we became Christians — a desire to please ourselves rather than God.

That pull begins in a subtle way but it can grow to a strong urging in another of the three areas of temptation.

Coveting

Do you have a spirit of longing to possess whatever you see? After you've been shopping, do mental images of items you knew you couldn't afford linger in your mind? Do you experience an enticement that insists you must have them anyway? This is coveting, the lust of the eye, and it is another form of temptation, a delusion. It causes us to think that happiness can be found in things. We're led to believe falsely that what we see with our eyes is what counts — clothes, jewelry, houses, cars, furniture, gadgets. Moral values or the standards of God are less important. The outward appearance is everything.

One woman in her mid-twenties described her compulsion to buy clothes. She worked downtown in a large city where she saw how fashions changed by what was displayed in store windows. She was surrounded by people wearing the latest styles. Her thoughts centered on clothes as she drove to and from work and plagued her mind as she prepared dinner. Her lunch hours and weekends were spent shopping. Relentlessly a voice in her thoughts bade her to buy — and she did — until her closet was overflowing. She said, "I can't afford them, but I feel so good when I'm buying. Yet I know I can't begin to wear all the clothes. This habit is causing me financial problems. Why do I buy, buy, buy?"

Doesn't her problem remind you of the woman in the letter who was compelled to eat, eat, eat? Temptation has this compelling persuasion urging us to satisfy our appetites. When we say yes and give in to the enticement to eat and buy whatever we see, we sin. Entrapped by the lust of the eye we are tempted to succumb to the related sins of envying and coveting. We develop a yearning to own and possess even what belongs to others.

Pride

Be careful. Maybe you're not tempted in either of these two areas — the desire of the flesh or the lust of the eyes. But what about pride? Do you feel an urge to be a superior Somebody? Is the motivating force of your life an allurement to display intellectual or creative ability, or to have applause and recognition for your achievements? Is it your desire to have your name known in social circles? Are you ever tempted, like Andrea in Tolstoy's *War and Peace*, to think, "For a little bit of glory I'd give up friends and family"?

If your temptation is to experience recognition or impress others with your importance, what do you need to make yourself look good?

Some years ago a young Christian woman sat in the seat next to me as we were driving around the city. On one particular street the houses were mansions — landscaped with flowering bushes and winding walkways. As she gazed at the stateliness of the neighborhood, she said, "This is what I want — to be the woman of the house in one of these mansions — entertaining lavishly — with all the comforts — and beautiful things everywhere! Wherever I go, I want people to say, 'There she is.' " This dear lady was determined!

Her desire was more than a little girl's "let's pretend." For twenty years I saw her strive to live in that elite neighborhood. She pressured her husband. She worked two jobs. She was consumed with a burning desire to hear, "There she is, the woman of the house in that prestigious neighborhood." To be able to boast about where she lived was her way of elevating herself above others. It was an entrapment of the pride of life. In her climb upward she neglected and disregarded God. Her all-consuming desire was to promote self.

Pride is a pitfall. It's often related to greed. Paul wrote a warning to young Timothy:

> People who want to get rich fall into temptation and a trap and into many foolish and harmful devices that plunge men into ruin and destruction. For the love of money is the root of all kinds of evil. Some people, eager for money, have wandered from the faith and pierced themselves with many griefs (1 Timothy 6:9,10).

Let's summarize these struggles with our enemies. We are tempted through our natural desires — God-created desires designed to help us survive and experience the sensation of pleasure. Food, sex, beauty and potential are all gifts from Him. Temptation entices us to fulfill these desires in the wrong way or to go beyond the limit God has established.

Mental Conflicts

Temptation is a mental struggle. It is aroused as we gaze at forbidden fruit, fan our imagination, or go to certain places. For example, viewing the television commercial of Oreos Cookies and Cream stimulated my friend's idea to drive to the store and get some. Window-shopping and looking at mansions induced lust and pride in two other women. Agreeing to meet an old boyfriend could ignite the flame of sexual desire. When do you think the peasant woman of Sychar took her first step toward evil? When she deliberately encouraged temptation by nourishing unwholesome sexual desires.

During temptation our love is vulnerable. Love for God can be extinguished as quickly as love for pleasure heightens. We find our hearts pitted against God as love for self increases. We mumble, "I don't care what God thinks. I want the ice cream...the clothes...the house...the boyfriend." Our thoughts influence our affections. Our affections influence our will. When we say "I will" to temptation, we choose to walk away from God and into sin. We become slaves to food...to lust...to pride.

Behind the Scenes

Our enemy is Satan. He is powerful. He uses allurement in temptation, dangling the artificial tinsel that dazzles our eyes and dulls our senses. The Bible calls him the tempter (Matthew 4:3), and the one who entices us (1 Corinthians 7:5). He deceitfully sells us his wares, appealing to our sinful nature.

Remember how Satan enticed Eve? In Genesis 3:5,6, a beguiling Satan said, "For God knows that when you eat of it your eyes will be opened, and you will be like God, knowing good and evil. When the woman saw that the fruit of the tree was good and pleasing to the eye, and also desirable for gaining wisdom, she took some and ate it." Attempting to satisfy the desire of the flesh, the lust of her eye, and her pride, she attained what Satan promised — but at the expense of disobeying God. She paid a high price.

Master of Deceit

A beautiful being, Satan lures women in the same deceitful way today. He just changes the falsehood to match the situation. Paul says, "For Satan himself masquerades as an angel of light" (2 Corinthians 11:14). Craftily he suggests, "Go see your old boyfriend. He needs your help. Be a witness of God's love and power to him." Or he says subtly, "Buy the fashionable clothes — God wants you to be a contemporary Christian." He smartly hums, "Work hard and long for the mansion. You could entertain God's people in its rooms some day."

How well do you know this enemy? Take a good look at him. He's famous for his disguises.

As we've seen, Satan typically bombards us with subtle suggestions. But other times he attacks us fiercely, as he did Peter. On the night before His crucifixion, Jesus warned Peter that Satan desired to sift him like wheat (Luke 22:31). A few hours later Peter was overcome when Satan tempted him to deny his Lord — three times in the same evening. Peter can warn us with the authority that comes from personal experience: "Your enemy, the devil, prowls around like a roaring lion, looking for someone to devour" (1 Peter 5:8).

Our enemy actively works to oppose confession of our faith in Christ. Along with instilling fearful thoughts when we try to witness, Satan distracts our attention from Christ with gossip, pleasure and prideful thoughts. He attempts to draw us back to our former ways, to block our effectiveness and to hinder our service.

Does Satan nag you with nostalgia for the good old days? Does he remind you of your former sinful life, suggesting you are not worthy to serve God? Beware. He is out to deceive you, to discredit you and to destroy your walk with the Lord in any way he can.

When a new Christian was asked to open her home for a Bible study, she said, "How could I dare open the Bible in our home? Our lives and our home formerly had a reputation for immorality." Satan desired to tie her to the past with this false guilt and to keep the light of the gospel from shining. It was a struggle for her to overcome this mentality.

Master of Destruction

Satan employs other tactics, too. He wants the body of believers weakened so that the church as a whole will cease to be an effective witness. His objective is to break up unity and loving fellowship among individuals. His method is to tempt us to hang on to resentment toward those in the church who have wronged us (2 Corinthians 2:11).

Like a master craftsman, Satan stirs up our prideful desires and weaves pieces of gossip through our imaginations. His twist of deceit forms a distorted picture of another believer in our minds.

For instance, while I am ironing, my mind is free to roam. Satan seems to perch on the edge of my ironing board, firing questions at me such as, "What are you going to do about Mary? You *saw* that she led the Bible study quite well. You *heard* somewhere that she is the kind of woman who wants to take over. Don't you *imagine* she wants your position?" Our minds become cluttered with these negative thoughts.

"The whole world is under the control of the evil one" (1 John 5:19). He now uses the world — not the physical, geographical world — but the philosophical world systems — to promote his evil principles and ambitions. Look at the greed and jealousies of nations and businesses. Reflect on the godless attitudes of mankind. You can see Satan's influence everywhere. He has stamped his logo in the heart of every person.

He wants us to love this world and set our affections on what he offers rather than on God and His kingdom. Since unbelievers are already in bondage to his evil system, his destructive efforts are directed toward God's people.

This explains why he entices the believer with tantalizing deceptions. He wants us to fall into sin. He wants to undermine our devotion to God. His consuming passion is to receive the worship that is due God alone.

Scripture gives us specific warnings about Satan's desire to tempt us in marriage and lead us to sin — we are especially vulnerable in the sexual area. Do you consistently express your love to your mate sexually? If you do, you are shielding yourself and your husband from Satan's seduction. The Christian concept of marriage encourages a couple to fulfill the natural passions of each other and not to restrict your sexual relations. Otherwise Satan will inflame the desire of the flesh and tempt you or your partner to participate in sexual immorality.

Paul gives only one reason to deny sexual expression. There's one priority that is higher than marriage — our intimacy with God in prayer. "Do not deprive each other except by mutual consent and for a time, so that you devote yourselves to prayer, then come together again so that Satan will not tempt you because of your lack of self-control" (1 Corinthians 7:5). Notice that the spiritual exception is by mutual consent and for a limited time. Resuming a normal sexual relationship is a necessity.

What keeps you apart? Is it an agreement for prayer? Or is it home responsibilities or selfish involvements?

Following the final session of a marriage conference, I met an attractive woman who told me her story of Satan's influence on her marriage. She said, "When I encountered God my life changed drastically. My new life in Christ was so exciting I attended three Bible studies a week, along with services all day Sunday. My husband, a successful professional man, at first ignored the change in my life. But unknown to me, my increasing involvement with religious activities began irritating him. He felt they interfered with our relationship. I started going to bed early. My strength was drained at the end of a long day. My husband became lonely. He missed sharing not only the late night hours with me but also the warmth of my presence in bed with him in the morning — I was up before sunrise, praying and studying. My devotion to Christ was genuine and my life bore fruit and others were nurtured. But Satan did a subtle work in our marriage."

She had been speaking softly and with clarity but then her voice cracked and tears filled her eyes when she said, "Neglecting my husband's need of sexual love and companionship provided Satan with a vulnerable man to lure toward another woman. My husband easily succumbed to an illicit affair. He yielded to an experienced woman — a worldly one who excited his fleshly desires. This may sound strange, but he saw me as a holy woman — a saint, set apart to reverence and be in awe of — not to love in a wifely way. Unaware of my husband's feelings and his image of me, I was shocked and devastated when I discovered his affair."

A woman devoted to Christ is praiseworthy. But we are not lofty, holy objects. We are human, sexual women with the need to give and receive love and companionship in marriage. Rather than distancing your husband, why not move toward him in love and enrich your sexual life? This is a legitimate defense against the evil one and a demonstration of God's love in your heart.
How vital it is to be aware of temptation's guises. Guard yourself. We're in spiritual conflict daily. It's an ongoing battle against Satan, the world he rules and our natural desires. Christians are his target.

Working behind the scenes, Satan and his network of spirits lure us and instill evil thoughts of pleasure and personal fulfillment in our minds. We know that yielding to temptation builds barriers in our relationship with God, causes guilt feelings stemming from breaking God's standards, produces dissatisfaction, and leads to evil.

STEPS TO LIFELONG VITALITY:
PRINCIPLES FOR EXALTING GOD AND OPPOSING ENEMIES

You want to be able to recognize your enemies and to overcome temptation, right? Let me share some how-to's with you. Learning to exalt God is the dynamic for overcoming the kinds of temptation we're most prone to.

1. *Authority.* The death and resurrection of Jesus Christ defeated Satan and demonstrated his authority over him (see Ephesians 1:19-22, Hebrews 2:14).

As a believer, you have authority over Satan because you are in Christ Jesus (see Ephesians 2:6). This is a critical truth. Claim it.

2. *Resistance.* All believers are tempted. Yet God provides an escape (see 1 Corinthians 10:13). The power of the Holy Spirit is available to you when you obediently submit yourself to God. Then you can resist Satan aggressively by simply saying, "In the name of Christ, I command you to leave me alone." Be confident God will do the shoving — He knows we are feeble, and on our own we are destined to fail (see James 4:7).

3. *Stability.* Jesus Christ understands temptation because He was tempted like we are (see Hebrews 4:15). Stand your ground firmly when evil temptations entice you. Assert your NO (see Ephesians 6:13). You need not be a victim of evil. You have God's power, enabling you to overcome evil with good.

4. *Equipment.* Jesus responded to Satan's attack of temptation by quoting: "It is written." Satan was defeated by God's Word. After he failed in his effort to

entice Jesus to sin, Satan departed and left Jesus alone for a season (see Luke 4:4,8,10).

5. *Prevention*. Guard your thought life. Satan is battling to control your mind, to deceive you concerning the truth of God, and to entice you through your thoughts to sin (see Romans 12:2).

Refuel your inner self daily with God's thoughts (see Psalm 119:11).

Refuse to look at things which induce evil thoughts (see Romans 13:14).

Reject plans that you know will tempt you to sin (see 1 Corinthians 6:18).

Be forgiving. Holding grudges gives Satan a foothold into your life (see Ephesians 4:27).

Love your husband. Expressing love sexually wards off Satan's temptation to immorality (see 1 Corinthians 7:5).

Pray for deliverance. "And lead us not into temptation, but deliver us from the evil one" (Matthew 6:13).

Pray for protection from unknown circumstances which could become evil allurement.

Pray also for our leaders who are combating Satan's powers. In Psalm 10, David teaches us that evil spirits influence world leaders and that wicked spirits are opposed by prayer.

Be alert. Watch for the camouflaged presence of the enemy. He is continually seeking someone to attack (see 1 Peter 5:8).

Rebuke the enemy. When Satan incites evil thinking in me — while I'm ironing or sleeping restlessly, or when I'm alone and free to daydream — I quote ALOUD the verse, "Casting down imaginations, and every high thing that exalteth itself against the knowledge of God, and bringing into captivity every thought to the obedience of Christ" (2 Corinthians 10:5, KJV).

Finally, remember that Satan tempts believers subtly and aggressively. Don't be led astray by seeking spiritual answers through the occult or other false teachings. These only lead to disillusionment and disobedience to God's Word (see Deuteronomy 18:10-12).

6. *Witness.* Even if Satan intensifies the battle against you, be faithful to confess Christ. You'll fulfill your earthly spiritual task by talking about Him wherever you go (see Acts 1:8).

You want to be a fruitful witness. You want to exalt God, making Him Lord of your life as a way of life. These dynamics can certainly revitalize your daily walk. Apply these principles for opposing Satan and resisting every temptation you encounter. Victory will become your trademark. Pleasure-seeking is filled with dissatisfaction, but you'll discover that there *are* ways to resist the pull toward temptation and overindulgence.

As the psalmist expressed it, "You have made known to me the path of life; you will fill me with joy in your presence, with eternal pleasures at your right hand" (Psalm 16:11).

8
Am I Pulling The Right Strings?

Yielding to the Spirit is
the dynamic for exercising true inner power

Who is the boss in your life? Is it an overbearing employer, a manipulating lover, or a domineering relative? Are you like the victim in this classic portrait of a woman who is bent on being in control?

Donna had recently become aware of the subtle domination. Nervously running her fingers through her hair, she described her mother's possessive hold on her. It was having a devastating effect on her marriage of nine months.

Donna spoke softly at first, as though she was afraid someone might hear her. "I don't know what to do about my mother. I know I love her, and I want to be good to her." Then in a higher pitched voice she said, "But I wish she would just move away or leave me alone. She's always there. As close as my shadow. When I walk in the door after work, the telephone is ringing. She's checking on me, asking me questions about my day just like I was a child. Or she's telling me all the bad things my father did that day to annoy her. After dinner she stops by the house, just when my husband and I are starting to relax. She even calls me at work and tells me little pieces of nonsense."

Her voice grew stronger and she punched the air with her fist. "My life is not my own. My mother is interfering with my marriage and my work. I feel her hovering over me everywhere, even in the privacy of our bedroom. It's difficult to make love — her invisible presence is there."

With tears flooding her eyes, Donna described her husband's response. "He told me I must cut the strings of attachment and set up some boundaries with my mother. Otherwise, he was not going to show up at home until late at night, or not at all. Yet, I can't break the ties. I'm indebted to her. She paid for our wedding out of her own savings and borrowed money to buy us a car for our wedding gift. She has told me over and over how much she hates my father. I'm her only child and if she didn't have me, she would have no-body."

The Struggle for Power

Donna's mother subtly used indebtedness in an effort to dominate and control her daughter. This is just one of the many types of power struggles that go on around us and within us all the time. Most of these are insidious and obscure. When we were children, though, the power struggles were more obvious. The largest, most aggressive child ruled by force. If we wanted to play with the forceful one, we were coerced into playing *her* way. But we did not like it any more than Donna liked what her mother was doing.

Through trial and error we often discovered ways other than physical force to withstand and equalize power. Or, we found ways to gain our own control. When we gave the bigger, more aggressive girl her favorite-colored lollipop, she stopped hitting us and played our way. We learned to play the power game at an early age. Some of us perfected the game, sometimes even becoming masters at it.

The one who possesses power either has exercised enough force to get his own way, or has been delegated the authority legitimately. Sometimes he or she is the persuasive and influential one who brings about changes in a social group.

I'm reminded of one particular socialite in our city. She was recently the victim of the cunning power of her social "boss." As a volunteer, she had set her sights on the top position — chairperson of the three-day annual fund raiser for one of the hospitals. It was an enviable position. Status. Recognition. And power. She'd be responsible to direct hundreds of volunteers. For *fifteen years* she worked in the fund-raising event, volunteering for all the tedious, unglamorous jobs. Year by year, she moved slowly through the ranks of the hierarchy toward the top position.

Finally she was ready. She "deserved" the chairpersonship. But that year the new president of the women's board, whose husband was an influential medical doctor, changed the hierarchy structure, and appointed a personal friend to that coveted position. None of the volunteer's hard work of fifteen years paid off.

What would you do in this situation? Accept the disappointment, sulk, fight back, or join the power game and find a subtle, deceitful way to defeat the boss, the president of the women's board?

Why do we give in to these bosses? There can be several reasons. If that boss can hurt us physically, monetarily or emotionally, we respond to that person's demands out of fear. We may be prompted by respect if we recognize someone's legitimate authority. Or we may choose voluntarily to accept the offer of a powerful persuader.

Our employers and the government are obvious powerful forces and authorities. We give in and type the late report for the boss for the sake of money; we make out our tax forms for Uncle Sam so we won't be financially penalized or have our reputation damaged.

You meet these bosses at every turn, and you fantasize your own magic to dethrone the power over you. *If only my boss were transferred*, you daydream. *If only the president of the women's organization were replaced.* When such dreams develop, they result in expending your energy, fighting the authority figure. The goal can escalate to striving for your own power. Becoming the boss can captivate our hearts and entangle us in a prideful power net.

The Pursuit of Power

Achieving power is the goal of *How To Make A Habit of Succeeding*, by Mark R. Douglas. He says that an attitude of thinking highly of yourself — considering yourself better than others — is paramount. Dressing to impress the right people, asserting yourself and refusing to say no are some of the recommended power tactics. Deceitfulness and manipulation are mentioned as the most effective power tools.

The epitome of this type of power manipulation is false advertising. Who of us has not been drawn by attractive packaging and irresistible promises, only to discover inferior merchandise and disappointing results?

Flattery, saying what others want to hear, is a familiar scheme for gaining power. What throws us off guard more than compliments about our appearance or intelligence? Remember your last experience with a man who tried to get what he wanted from you with smooth sounding words? He may have wanted your money, he may have wanted your body — or both. Many teen-age girls and love-starved, lonely women are betrayed by the flattering words of clever men.

Through her tears, one broken-hearted woman related, "He said he loved me, and would respect me if I gave him my body. But I was used like a toy and then discarded for a new one. He barely acknowledges me and now has no interest in me or our unborn child."

Uncontrolled natural desires can give rise to a thirst for power to gratify self. The disciples of Jesus were not immune. When Jesus was facing death His closest companions discussed power and argued about who would possess the most. It seems their main interest was in what they could gain personally from their association with Jesus.

Men may use aggressiveness or flattery to gain power, but women have their ways of attaining it, too. A little girl learns to woo her father with the seemingly innocent but obvious *power words*, "Oh, Daddy, I love you. I wish you would buy me this doll."

Grown-up women are capable of similar manipulation tactics directed toward boyfriends, husbands and competitors in the market place. Sexual flirtations — a cute smile, a lift of the skirt, a twist of the ankle, and hundreds of other sexual messages — are womanly ploys.

Flirtations in the context of marriage are legitimate, beneficial clues from a wife to a husband — hints that she is in the mood for making love. However, tantalizing her husband with sexual delight for her own self-centered purposes — wrapping her husband around her little finger — is a manipulative feminine power device. Any woman who uses her sexuality to gain favors or to get her own way is tossing truth aside. She misuses her specially created womanhood for deceitful gain.

Women often use sexuality for power purposes in the workplace as well as in the bedroom. The color, cut, fabric of a dress, blouse, sweater, skirt or slacks, can attract attention and give her entree to influential people. A woman pursuing power may or may not use her opportunities in sexual immorality. Many cleverly mislead with sexual suggestions, spoken and unspoken, exploiting men for their own advantage.

Remember Delilah who beguiled Samson so she could gain important information about his superhuman strength? Other women like her are described in Proverbs. They trick a man for selfish purposes. Proverbs 7:21 says, "With persuasive words she led him astray; she seduced him with her smooth talk." Men are not the only smooth talkers. Women can be just as selfishly ambitious as men.

Some women use tears rather than sexual suggestions to gain an edge with men when they want something. Do you cry easily? Is it from a tender heart? Are your tears expressions of concern or joy for others? Or are your tears power tools?

I remember a girl who lived on my dorm floor in college. She was a large girl, with a baby face and big blue eyes. When we gathered in her room one evening for prayer time she said, "You know I was failing one of my courses, but I think I got the professor's sympathy today and I'm confident he'll give me a passing grade."

She gave a quick giggle, then added, "I went in to talk to him and I let tears roll down my cheeks and onto his desk. He was so concerned he pulled out his own handkerchief and handed it to me, and said he would look at my work again and see what he could do."

There are many beguiling ways to be in control. Have you ever observed a capable woman feign helplessness in order to get others to care for her needs?

Have you known a woman to use sickness for her advantage? I once observed a smart woman who powerfully controlled three store clerks at one time. She appeared unable to find items or to make decisions. The clerks catered to her every whim. They searched through the racks and in the back room for a special item just to please the "helpless" customer.

Women entering the workplace encounter a different form of power struggle and may find themselves using different types of manipulative tactics. We find ambitious women and jealous men competing for the top positions. Will we fall into the trap of desiring a position so strongly that we will use wrong methods to get it? There is a danger that we'll take advantage of an upper hand in the marketplace or earn enough money that we think we should have the say-so in our marriage. Power is addictive. Those with power tend to maneuver others in order to gain personal pleasure and security.

The power god is attractive to men and women alike. Both want money and prestige. In the grip of worldly power, both sexes are tempted to go overboard to achieve success. Too often, leaders become intoxicated with their own power and neglect caring for the ones they rule. Society's bosses tend to close their eyes and ears to those who cry and suffer — the very ones they once loved.

Cheryl Forbes raises a probing question in her book, *Are We Victims of the Religion of Power?* She traces the desire for power to its beginning.

> From the first day of creation men and women have faced the problem of power. It was the desire to be powerful — to be like God — that caused Adam and Eve to disobey the Lord. Satan understood from first hand experience how great was the call of power. He fell from Heaven because he longed to be greater than he was....

The Patriarchs, Judges, Priests, Kings, Prophets
of the Old Testament and Apostles of the new,
Paul included, were imperfect men who struggled
against becoming children of the lesser god,
power, to become the children of the greater God
of Power.[1]

Ultimate Power

Each of us lives under the authority of an earthly
power, a boss, and each of us, in turn, has our sphere
of influence or area where we are in charge. We may
legitimately attain a high level of power by hard work
and proper degrees or appointments. No matter how
we struggle to move through the ranks, though, there
are limits to power. No one has it all. Only God holds
ultimate power.

One of King David's prayers points to the true source
of power. "Yours, O LORD, is the greatness and the
power and the glory and the majesty and the splendor,
for everything in heaven and earth is yours. Yours, O
LORD, is the kingdom; you are exalted as head over
all. Wealth and honor come from you; you are the
ruler of all things. In your hands are strength and
power to exalt and give strength to all. Now, our God,
we give you thanks, and praise your glorious name"
(1 Chronicles 29:11-13).

God's creation reveals His ultimate power — He
created the heavens and the earth from nothing. Then
He formed the first man and woman. He established
the life principle that we participate in as we bear new
life.

Transforming Power

Hand in hand with the might of creation is the
power of the resurrection. The apostle Paul refers to
it often. "That power is like the working of His mighty

strength, which He exerted in Christ when He raised Him from the dead" (Ephesians 1:19,20).

When we become God's child, the presence of God takes up residence in our heart by means of the person of the Holy Spirit.

He is our true Inner Dynamic.

He is the source of power that enables us to live fulfilling and productive lives for God. His power helps us express these dynamics of a woman's life which we have looked at in previous chapters:

- to reach our potential
- to know who we are
- to grow in maturity
- to control anxiety
- to dispel depression
- to master anger
- to overcome our enemy

Now we turn to the last one: *experiencing strength.* It begins with yielding to His control — doing what God commands in His Word as our part in living the Christian life. As we read or hear God's Word the Holy Spirit faithfully convicts our hearts of wrongdoing. Sometimes conviction occurs as we hear a testimony or listen to a sermon.

A woman I met some years ago in New Castle, England, is a good example of how a woman *obediently* responded to God's convicting power. After Dave finished preaching, she walked to the front of the auditorium and said, "Mrs. Burnham, I need to talk to you." She was crying so hard it was difficult for me to understand her.

I said, "Mary, what is troubling you?"

She said, "I've been married two years and already I am a 'nog' ". It took me a moment to grasp her problem. Then I realized she was referring to the same problem of "nagging" that we American women have.

She continued, "I nog my husband when he wants to see his friends on Saturday. I argue and beg him to stay home and do things around the apartment. I think he should help me clean, and he should do some repairs. And there's another thing. A few months ago I told my sister I would care for her two-year-old boy after school until bedtime. I did this against my husband's wishes and our arguing intensified. We have argued so much I don't know if he even loves me anymore."

Tears came in a flood again. Then she said, "I saw my selfishness tonight in your husband's sermon — I saw my domineering ways. I need God's help to stop nogging and trying to control him. I need to start loving him."

That night, Mary chose to stop living a defeated life. Confessing her wrongdoing, she experienced God's power of love as it flowed into her heart again. She discovered that yielding to God releases His power. He enables us to do what is right and brings us fulfillment in our inner life.

Where do we need God's power to transform us more than in our close relationships at home? The conflict is that we tend to try to control those we live with. But we need to draw on God's power to love our family members.

His Spirit can make a difference in your interpersonal relationships. Spiritual fruit (see Galatians 5:22,23) can be cultivated in your home life. How is this done?

• *Kindness* is offering a tender touch. It's a word softly spoken for the one who is weary. It's encouragement for the one who is discouraged.

• *Patience* is unselfish giving during the nursing and diaper stage. It's listening to teens, beyond words, to the needs of the heart. It's being there for your husband when he needs you most.

• *Joy* is participating in each other's interests.

• *Self-control* is consideration during disagreements.

• *Faithfulness* is a warm, responsive presence when other family members depend on you — even when their hearts grow away from you.

Your family members may include an elderly mother or father-in-law. Maybe you have a handicapped child or a disabled sister, besides your husband and children — all living under one roof. It seems as though each fruit of the Spirit is designed especially for meeting the needs of women in nurturing and care-taking roles.

Are you a career woman or a mother working out of your home? Do you recognize God's power working through you to accomplish His plan? Whatever work you do, you can do it for Him. No task is too menial to be unimportant to Him, or so prestigious that it will impress Him. He wants to do a powerful work through you, whatever your calling. Guard against playing power games at work; rather ask God to demonstrate *His* power through your talents and abilities.

Everyone is gifted. God created us with an assortment of talents and gifts. When this diversity is integrated into the body of Christ, a balance is achieved (see 1 Corinthians 12 and Ephesians 4). You may have a special skill in art or music. Or maybe you are quick to gain insight, or capable of explaining and teaching. Perhaps you are good at organizing and leading. Someone else may be creative. Or you might be prone to offer an appropriate word of encouragement or to reach out to those suffering.

Your specific capabilities map out your line of duty in the world and in the body of Christ (2 Corinthians 10:13). The Holy Spirit empowers you to fulfill it. Once you discover your special ministry, ask God for opportunities to develop it.

Witnessing Power

There is one task God gives to every one of His disciples. We are commanded to share the gospel message. Jesus said, "Therefore go and make disciples of all nations" (Matthew 28:19,20). Before He returned to heaven, Jesus promised that He would enable us to witness by giving us the power of the Holy Spirit (see Acts 1:8).

Are you frightened at the thought of telling others that Christ died for them? It might help you to remember what Paul said: "For the message of the cross is foolishness to those who are perishing, but to us who are being saved, it is the power of God" (2 Corinthians).

I can remember an occasion when I felt foolish about witnessing. I attended a party in an exclusive area of our city with six other hospital volunteers — I had felt accepted by them.

We were all sitting around in comfortable chairs after lunch, talking, when the discussion turned to what it means to be "born again." It was popular at that time to scoff at the phrase, yet I felt compelled to explain its meaning from the biblical context and to share with them my own experience of being born again by the Spirit of God. All six of them were surprised and curious.

The kindest lady attempted to defend me. She said, "I think what you really mean is you're born again with a new, fresh perspective of life, like noticing petals for the first time on a flower after you've been sick." I began to feel warm all over and very uncomfortable, but I said, "No, it is more than that. To be born again is to become inwardly new by faith in Christ."

Then the one who was most prominent in the community said, "Oh, Sue, you're really making a fool of yourself today." Her legs had been comfortably tucked beneath her on the sofa, but at that moment she shifted her position, put her feet on the floor, and leaned forward to look directly into my face. She mockingly said, "I can't believe you'd think that way."

The atmosphere grew cool and shortly thereafter I said my goodbyes. Driving home I at first felt lonely and rejected. But by the time I arrived, I was feeling a warm sense of God's presence and comfort deep inside. It was the result of yielding to His will.

When we witness to people about Jesus Christ we rely on the convicting power of the Holy Spirit to reveal God's viewpoint of sin to them. He shows them their need of a Savior. I had to depend on the Holy Spirit to convict my friends just as He convicted people at Pentecost when Peter preached and three thousand people responded to his message (Acts 2:41).

In his book, *Loving God*, Chuck Colson describes the dramatic experience he had after hearing about his friend's conversion:

> But that night when I left my friend and sat alone in my car, my own sin — not just Watergate, but the evil deep within — was thrust before me by the conviction of the Holy Spirit forcefully and painfully. For the first time in my life I felt unclean. Yet I could not run away. I was as helpless as the thief nailed to that cross and what I saw within me was so ugly I could do nothing but cry out to God for help.[2]

Power for Guidance

When we obey God and depend on Him to help us — even when others call us foolish — His power is released. It may be His power of conviction, or it may be His power of strength when we are weak. Or it can be His power for guidance when we seek answers.

I am reminded of a time in my life when I learned this lesson. The Bible study ministry in our Midwestern church evolved from a discouraging beginning, a time when I was pressed to depend on God.

One cold January day a woman called to inquire if I would teach her and her unbelieving friend the Bible. I had never led a Bible study, but I said, "Yes, I'm certain I can work it out."

I didn't know a thing about effective Bible study methods. So I prepared ten pages of notes and planned to tell them everything I had written down. On the following Wednesday I dropped off our four-year-old son, Jonathan, at his nursery school and drove ten miles on icy roads to the woman's home. I spread my notes out on the kitchen table. But as it turned out, I only gave a thimbleful of the lesson. There were children playing at our feet, telephone calls, and interruptions of all sorts — the entire two hours.

My heart sank with disappointment when I looked at the clock. It was time for me to go. I had to pick up Jonathan. When I arrived home, one of my daughters was on the sofa crying because of an incident at school that afternoon. And *Why today?* flashed through my mind.

After listening to her and offering comfort, I took her with me to the grocery store before dinner. At the store a neighbor saw me and yelled out, "Your dog was running free in our yard this afternoon and I didn't appreciate it." Her unfriendly tone was within listening range for all the customers. I fretted, "How did our puppy get loose?" And again asked myself, *Why today?*

I felt embarrassed, frustrated, discouraged. As I prepared dinner, I dialogued with myself, then the Lord. *Sue, why trouble yourself with that study?* Then, "Oh, Lord, what do you want? Do you really want me to try to lead a study like this?"

As I rinsed the dishes after dinner, thoughts on how to remedy each specific event crossed my mind. I formulated a plan for inviting the two women to come to my home where I could supervise their children, Jonathan, and our puppy.

As my thoughts raced, I became confident I could search for an effective method to study with them. God's power of peace settled in my heart. Discouragement disappeared. I allowed God to turn the incidences of that frustrating afternoon around, and a Bible study ministry began. My dependence on God released His Spirit's power.

I found the strength and guidance I needed to try a new venture. The ministry grew and flourished. It came about by God's power working through our lives — women yielded to Him and dependent on Him. We came to see that the truth of the Scripture that says He "is able to do immeasurably more than all we ask or imagine according to His power that is at work within us" (Ephesians 3:20).

Evaluate The Power Factors In Your Life

How do you use your power? Selfishly? With love? For the glory of God? Here is a checklist to help you evaluate the power factors in your life. It's a good idea to look at this every few weeks to check up on your developing personal power structure. Ask yourself:

Do I attempt to control others by any of these deceit-ful tactics?

Yes   No

[ ] [ ] Manipulation.

[ ] [ ] Buying Favors.

[ ] [ ] Feminine beguilement.

How do I need the power of the Holy Spirit to work in my life?

[ ] To heal a relationship.

[ ] To guide me.

[ ] To comfort me.

[ ] To convict and draw a loved one to Christ.

What is holding back the power of the Holy Spirit in my life?

[ ] Giving in to sin.

[ ] Controlling my own life rather than depending on God.

[ ] Controlling others for selfish purposes or by evil tactics.

[ ] Grieving the Holy Spirit (Ephesians 4:30).

Let me encourage you to take the first step now. Will you humble yourself before God? Confess and lay your selfish, controlling techniques at His feet. Boldly ask God to release His power in you today.

Alexander Solzhenitsyn said,

> Power is a poison well known for thousands of years. If only no one were ever to acquire material power over others! But to the human

being who has faith in some force that holds
dominion over all of us, and who is therefore
conscious of his own limitations, power is not
necessarily fatal. For those, however, who are
unaware of any higher sphere, it is deadly poison.
For them there is no antidote.[3]

Do you want to become a woman of strength? You
can — through Christ, the true source of power.

This is my prayer for you:

Heavenly Father, I pray that out of Your glorious
riches You may, with power through Your Spirit,
strengthen the person now reading this in her
inner being, so that Christ may dwell in her heart
through faith. And I pray that she, being rooted
and established in love, may have power, together
with all the saints, to grasp how wide and long
and high and deep is the love of Christ, and to
know this love that surpasses knowledge — that
she may be filled to the measure of all the fullness
of God (from Ephesians 3:16-19).

NOTES

Chapter 1
1. James Dobson, *Straight Talk to Men and Their Wives* (Waco, Texas: Word Inc., 1984), p. 154.
2. *Newsweek,* October 15, 1984,

Chapter 3
1. Alexander Solzhenitsyn, *The Gulag Archipelago 1918-1956* (New York: Harper and Row Publishers, 1973), p. 591.

Chapter 5
1. Don Baker and Emery Nester, *Depression* (Portland, Oregon: Multnomah Press, 1983), p. 7.
2. Maggie Scarf, *Psychology Today* (April, 1979).

Chapter 7
1. M. Scott Peck, *People of the Lie* (New York: Simon and Schuster, 1983), pp. 190-91.

Chapter 8
1. Cheryl Forbes, *The Religion of Power* (Grand Rapids, Michigan: Zondervan Publishing House, 1983), pp. 109, 135.
2. Charles W. Colson, *Loving God* (Grand Rapids, Michigan: Zondervan Publishing House, 1983), p. 121.
3. Alexander Solzhenitsyn, *The Gulag Archipelago 1918-1956* (New York: Harper and Row Publishers, 1973), p. 147.

APPENDIX

HAVE YOU HEARD
OF THE
FOUR SPIRITUAL LAWS?

Just as there are physical laws that govern the physical universe, so are there spiritual laws which govern your relationship with God.

LAW ONE

GOD LOVES YOU, AND OFFERS A WONDERFUL PLAN FOR YOUR LIFE.

GOD'S LOVE

"For God so loved the world, that He gave His only begotten Son, that whoever believes in Him should not perish, but have eternal life." (John 3:16).

GOD'S PLAN

(Christ speaking) "I came that they might have life, and might have it abundantly" (that it might be full and meaningful) (John 10:10).

> Why is it that most people are
> not experiencing the abundant life?
> Because. . .

LAW TWO

MAN IS SINFUL AND SEPARATED FROM GOD, THUS, HE CANNOT KNOW AND EXPERIENCE GOD'S LOVE AND PLAN FOR HIS LIFE.

MAN IS SINFUL

"For all have sinned and fall short of the glory of God" (Romans 3:23).

Man was created to have fellowship with God; but, because of his own stubborn self-will, he chose to go his own independent way and fellowship with God was broken. This self-will, characterized by an attitude of active rebellion or passive indifference, is an evidence of what the Bible calls sin.

MAN IS SEPARATED

"For the wages of sin is death" (spiritual separation from God) (Romans 6:23).

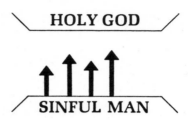

This diagram illustrates that God is holy and man is sinful. A great gulf separates the two. The arrows illustrate that man is continually trying to reach God and the abundant life through his own effort, such as a good life, philosophy or religion.

> The Third Law explains the only
> way to bridge this gulf. . .

LAW THREE

JESUS CHRIST IS GOD'S ONLY PROVISION FOR MAN'S SIN. THROUGH HIM YOU CAN KNOW AND EXPERIENCE GOD'S LOVE AND PLAN FOR YOUR LIFE.

HE DIED IN OUR PLACE

"But God demonstrates His own love toward us, in that while we were yet sinners, Christ died for us" (Romans 5:8).

HE ROSE FROM THE DEAD

"Christ died for our sins. . .he was buried. . .He was raised on the third day according to the Scriptures. . .He appeared to Peter, then to the twelve. After that He appeared to more than five hundred. . ." (I Corinthians 15:3-6).

HE IS THE ONLY WAY TO GOD

"Jesus said to him, 'I am the way, and the truth and the life; no one comes to the Father, but through Me'" (John 14:6).

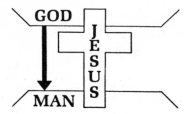

This diagram illustrates that God has bridged the gulf which separates us from Him by sending His Son, Jesus Christ, to die on the cross in our place to pay the penalty for our sins.

It is not enough to know these three laws nor even to give intellectual assent to them. . .

LAW FOUR

WE MUST INDIVIDUALLY **RECEIVE** JESUS CHRIST AS SAVIOR AND LORD; THEN WE CAN KNOW AND EXPERIENCE GOD'S LOVE AND PLAN FOR OUR LIVES.

WE MUST RECEIVE CHRIST

"But as many as received Him, to them He gave the right to become children of God, even to those who believe in His name" (John 1:12).

WE RECEIVE CHRIST THROUGH FAITH

"For by grace you have been saved through faith; and that not of your selves, it is a gift of God; not as a result of works, that no one should boast" (Ephesians 2:8,9).

When We Receive Christ, We Experience a New Birth

(Read John 3:1-8.)

WE RECEIVE CHRIST BY PERSONAL INVITATION

(Christ is speaking) "Behold, I stand at the door and knock; if anyone hears My voice and opens the door, I will come in to him" (Revelation 3:20).

Receiving Christ involves turning to God from self (repentance) and trusting Christ to come into our lives to forgive our sins and to make us the kind of people He wants us to be. Just to agree intellectually that Jesus Christ is the Son of God and that He died on the cross for our sins is not enough. Nor is it enough to have an emotional experience. We receive Jesus Christ by faith, as an act of the will.

These two circles represent two kinds of lives:

SELF-DIRECTED LIFE
S — Self is on the throne
† — Christ is outside the life
● — Interests are directed by self, often resulting in discord and frustration

CHRIST-DIRECTED LIFE
† — Christ is in the life and on the throne
S — Self is yielding to Christ
● — Interests are directed by Christ, resulting in harmony with God's plan

Which circle best represents your life?
Which circle would you like to have represent your life?
The following explains how you can receive Christ:

YOU CAN RECEIVE CHRIST RIGHT NOW BY FAITH THROUGH PRAYER

(Prayer is talking with God)

God knows your heart and is not so concerned with your words as He is with the attitude of your heart. The following is a suggested prayer:

"Lord Jesus, I need You. Thank You for dying on the cross for my sins. I open the door of my life and receive You as my Savior and Lord. Thank You for forgiving my sins and giving me eternal life. Take control of the throne of my life. Make me the kind of person You want me to be."

Does this prayer express the desire of your heart?

If it does, pray this prayer right now, and Christ will come into your life, as He promised.

HOW TO KNOW THAT CHRIST IS IN YOUR LIFE

Did you receive Christ into your life? According to His promise in Revelation 3:20, where is Christ right now in relation to you? Christ said that He would come into your life. Would He mislead you? On what authority do you know that God has answered your prayer? (The trustworthiness of God Himself and His Word).

THE BIBLE PROMISES ETERNAL LIFE TO ALL WHO RECEIVE CHRIST

"And the witness is this, that God has given us eternal life, and this life is in His Son. He who has the Son has the life; he who does not have the Son of God does not have the life. These things I have written to you who believe in the name of the Son of God, in order that you may know that you have eternal life" (I John 5:11-13).

Thank God often that Christ is in your life and that He will never leave you (Hebrews 13:5). You can know on the basis of His promise that Christ lives in you and that you have eternal life, from the very moment you invite Him in. He will not deceive you.

MEET WITH OTHER CHRISTIANS

The Christian life was not meant to be lived alone. God's Word admonishes us not to forsake "the assembling of ourselves together . . ." (Hebrews 10:25). Several logs burn brightly together; but put one aside on the cold hearth and the fire goes out. So it is with your relationship to other Christians. If you do not belong to a church, do not wait to be invited. Take the initiative; call the pastor of a nearby church where Christ is honored and His Word is preached. Start this week, and make plans to attend regularly.

Have You Made the Wonderful Discovery of the Spirit-Filled Life?

Every day can be an exciting adventure for the Christian who knows the reality of being filled with the Holy Spirit and who lives constantly, moment by moment, under His gracious direction.

The Bible tells us that there are three kinds of people:

NATURAL MAN (one who has not received Christ).

But a natural man does not accept the things of the Spirit of God; for they are foolishness to him, and he cannot understand them, because they are spiritually appraised (1 Corinthians 2:14).

SELF-DIRECTED LIFE
S—Self is on the throne
✝—Christ is outside the life
●—Interests are directed by self, often resulting in discord and frustration

SPIRITUAL MAN (one who is directed and empowered by the Holy Spirit).

But he who is spiritual appraises all things . . . (1 Corinthians 2:15).

CHRIST-DIRECTED LIFE
✝—Christ is in the life and on the throne
S—Self is yielding to Christ
●—Interests are directed by Christ, resulting in harmony with God's plan

CARNAL MAN (one who has received Christ, but who lives in defeat because he trusts in his own efforts to live the Christian life).

And I, brethren, could not speak to you as to spiritual men, but as to carnal men, as to babes in Christ. I gave you milk to drink, not solid food; for you were not yet able to receive it. Indeed, even now you are not yet able, for you are still carnal. For since there is jealousy and strife among you, are you not fleshly, and are you not walking like mere men? (1 Corinthians 3:1-3).

SELF-DIRECTED LIFE
S—Self is on the throne
†—Christ dethroned and not allowed to direct the life
●—Interests are directed by self, often resulting in discord and frustration

Three key truths introduce God's provision, His require-ment and His promise for the Spirit-filled life.

1 God has provided for us an abundant and fruitful Christian life.

Jesus said, "I came that they might have life, and might have it abun-dantly" (John 10:10).

I am the vine, you are the branches; he who abides in Me, and I in him, he bears much fruit; for apart from Me you can do nothing (John 15:5).

But the fruit of the Spirit is love, joy, peace, patience, kindness, good-ness, faithfulness, gentleness, self-control; against such things there is no law (Galatians 5:22,23).

But you shall receive power when the Holy Spirit has come upon you; and you shall be My witnesses both in Jerusalem, and in all Judea and Samaria, and even to the remotest part of the earth (Acts 1:8).

THE SPIRITUAL MAN—Some personal traits which result from trusting God:

Christ-centered
Empowered by the Holy Spirit
Introduces others to Christ
Effective prayer life
Understands God's Word
Trusts God
Obeys God

Love
Joy
Peace
Patience
Kindness
Faithfulness
Goodness

The degree to which these traits are manifested in the life depends upon the extent to which the Christian trusts the Lord with every detail of his life, and upon his maturity in Christ. One who is only beginning to understand the ministry of the Holy Spirit should not be discouraged if he is not as fruitful as the more mature Christians who have known and experienced this truth for a longer period.

Why is it that most Christians are not experiencing the abundant life?

2 Carnal Christians cannot experience the abundant and fruitful Christian life.

The carnal man trusts in his own efforts to live the Christian life:

A. He is either uninformed about, or has forgotten, God's love, forgiveness, and power (Romans 5:8-10; Hebrews 10:1-25; 1 John 1; 2:1-3; 2 Peter 1:9; Acts 1:8).
B. He has an up-and-down spiritual experience.
C. He cannot understand himself—he wants to do what is right, but cannot.
D. He fails to draw upon the power of the Holy Spirit to live the Christian life (1 Corinthians 3:1-3; Romans 7:15-24; 8:7; Galatians 5:16-18).

THE CARNAL MAN—Some or all of the following traits may characterize the Christian who does not fully trust God:

Ignorance of his spiritual heritage
Unbelief
Disobedience
Loss of love for God and for others
Poor prayer life
No desire for Bible study
Legalistic attitude

Impure thoughts
Jealousy
Guilt
Worry
Discouragement
Critical spirit
Frustration
Aimlessness

(The individual who professes to be a Christian but who continues to practice sin should realize that he may not be a Christian at all, according to 1 John 2:3; 3:6,9; Ephesians 5:5).

The third truth gives us the only solution to this problem . . .

3 Jesus promised the abundant and fruitful life as the result of being filled (directed and empowered) by the Holy Spirit.

The Spirit-filled life is the Christ-directed life by which Christ lives His life in and through us in the power of the Holy Spirit (John 15).

A. One becomes a Christian through the ministry of the Holy Spirit, according to John 3:1-8. From the moment of spiritual birth, the Christian is indwelt by the Holy Spirit at all times (John 1:12; Colossians 2:9,10; John 14:16,17). *Though all Christians are indwelt by the Holy Spirit, not all Christians are filled (directed and empowered) by the Holy Spirit.*

B. The Holy Spirit is the source of the overflowing life (John 7:37-39).

C. The Holy Spirit came to glorify Christ (John 16:1-15). When one is filled with the Holy Spirit, he is a true disciple of Christ.

D. In His last command before His ascension, Christ promised the power of the Holy Spirit to enable us to be witnesses for Him (Acts 1:1-9).

How, then, can one be filled with the Holy Spirit?

We are filled (directed and empowered) by the Holy Spirit by faith; then we can experience the abundant and fruitful life which Christ promised to each Christian.

You can appropriate the filling of the Holy Spirit *right now* if you:

A. Sincerely desire to be directed and empowered by the Holy Spirit (Matthew 5:6; John 7:37-39).

B. Confess your sins.
By *faith* thank God that He *has* forgiven all of your sins—past, present and future—because Christ died for you (Colossians 2:13-15; 1 John 1; 2:1-3; Hebrews 10:1-17).

C. Present every area of your life to God (Romans 12:1,2).

D. By *faith* claim the fullness of the Holy Spirit, according to:
  1. HIS COMMAND—Be filled with the Spirit. "And do not get drunk with wine, for that is dissipation, but be filled with the Spirit" (Ephesians 5:18).
  2. HIS PROMISE—He will always answer when we pray according to His will. "And this is the confidence which we have before Him, that, if we ask anything according to His will, He hears us. And if we know that He hears us in whatever we ask, we know that we have the requests which we have asked from Him" (1 John 5:14,15).

Faith can be expressed through prayer . . .

How to pray in faith to be filled with the Holy Spirit

We are filled with the Holy Spirit by *faith* alone. However, true prayer is one way of expressing your faith. The following is a suggested prayer.

> "Dear Father, I need You. I acknowledge that I have been directing my own life and that, as a result, I have sinned against You. I thank You that You have forgiven my sins through Christ's death on the cross for me. I now invite Christ to take His place again on the throne of my life. Fill me with the Holy Spirit as You *commanded* me to be filled, and as You *promised* in Your Word that You would do if I asked in faith. I pray this in the name of Jesus. As an expression of my faith, I now thank You for directing my life and for filling me with the Holy Spirit."

Does this prayer express the desire of your heart? If so, bow in prayer and trust God to fill you with the Holy Spirit *right now.*

How to know that you are filled (directed and empowered) by the Holy Spirit

Did you ask God to fill you with the Holy Spirit? Do you know that you are now filled with the Holy Spirit? On what authority? (On the trustworthiness of God Himself and His Word: Hebrews 11:6; Romans 14:22,23).

Do not depend upon feelings. The promise of God's Word, not our feelings, is our authority. The Christian lives by faith (trust) in the trustworthiness of God Himself and His Word. This train diagram illustrates the relationship between *fact* (God and His Word), *faith* (our trust in God and His Word), and *feeling* (the result of our faith and obedience) (John 14:21).

The train will run with or without the caboose. However, it would be futile to attempt to pull the train by the caboose. In the same way, we, as Christians, do not depend upon feelings or emotions, but we place our faith (trust) in the trustworthiness of God and the promises of His Word.

How to walk in the Spirit

Faith (trust in God and in His promises) is the only means by which a Christian can live the Spirit-directed life. As you continue to trust Christ moment by moment:

A. Your life will demonstrate more and more of the fruit of the Spirit (Galatians 5:22,23) and will be more and more conformed to the image of Christ (Romans 12:2; 2 Corinthians 3:18).

B. Your prayer life and study of God's Word will become more meaningful.

C. You will experience His power in witnessing (Acts 1:8).

D. You will be prepared for spiritual conflict against the world (1 John 2:15-17); against the flesh (Galatians 5:16,17); and against Satan (1 Peter 5:7-9; Ephesians 6:10-13).

E. You will experience His power to resist temptation and sin (1 Corinthians 10:13; Philippians 4:13; Ephesians 1:19-23; 6:10; 2 Timothy 1:7; Romans 6:1-16).

Spiritual breathing

By faith you can continue to experience God's love and forgiveness. If you become aware of an area of your life (an attitude or an action) that is displeasing to the Lord, even though you are walking with Him and sincerely desiring to serve Him, simply thank God that He has forgiven your sins—past, present and future—on the basis of Christ's death on the cross. Claim His love and forgiveness by faith and continue to have fellowship with Him.

If you retake the throne of your life through sin—a definite act of disobedience—breathe spiritually.

Spiritual breathing (exhaling the impure and inhaling the pure) is an exercise in faith that enables you to continue to experience God's love and forgiveness.

1. *Exhale*—confess your sin. Agree with God concerning your sin and thank Him for His forgiveness of it, according to 1 John 1:9 and Hebrews 10:1-25. Confession involves repentance—a change in attitude and action.

2. *Inhale*—surrender the control of your life to Christ, and appropriate (receive) the fullness of the Holy Spirit by faith. Trust that He now directs and empowers you, according to the *command* of Ephesians 5:18, and the *promise* of 1 John 5:14,15.